# Hydrogen

## Other books in the Fueling the Future series:

# Hydrogen

David M. Haugen, *Book Editor*

Bonnie Szumski, *Publisher*
Helen Cothran, *Managing Editor*

**GREENHAVEN PRESS**

*An imprint of Thomson Gale, a part of The Thomson Corporation*

THOMSON
━━━━✳━━━━ ™
GALE

Detroit • New York • San Francisco • San Diego • New Haven, Conn. • Waterville, Maine • London • Munich

LIBRARY OF CONGRESS CATALOGING-IN-PUBLICATION DATA

Hydrogen / David M. Haugen, book editor.
   p. cm. — (Fueling the future)
     Includes bibliographical references and index.
   ISBN 0-7377-3592-9 (lib. : alk. paper)
   1. Hydrogen as fuel.  2. Hydrogen as fuel—Economic aspects.  I. Haugen, David M.,
1969–  II. Series.
   TP359.H8H93 2006
   665.8'1—dc22
                                                              2006043414

Printed in the United States of America

# Contents

## Chapter 3: How Feasible Is a Future Hydrogen Economy?

# Foreword

The wind farm at Altamont Pass in Northern California epitomizes many people's idea of wind power: Hundreds of towering white turbines generate electricity to power homes, factories, and businesses. The spinning turbine blades call up visions of a brighter future in which clean, renewable energy sources replace dwindling and polluting fossil fuels. The blades also kill over a thousand birds of prey each year. Every energy source, it seems, has its price.

The bird deaths at Altamont Pass make clear an unfortunate fact about all energy sources, including renewables: They have downsides. People want clean, abundant energy to power their modern lifestyles, but few want to pay the costs associated with energy production and use. Oil, coal, and natural gas contain high amounts of energy, but using them produces pollution. Commercial solar energy facilities require hundreds of acres of land and thus must be located in rural areas. Expensive and ugly transmission lines must then be run from the solar plants to the cities that need power. Producing hydrogen for fuel involves the use of dirty fossil fuels, tapping geothermal energy depletes ground water, and growing biomass for fuel ties up land that could be used to grow food. Hydroelectric power has become increasingly unpopular because dams flood vital habitats and kill wildlife and plants. Perhaps most controversial, nuclear power plants produce highly dangerous radioactive waste. People's reluctance to pay these environmental costs can be seen in the results of a 2006 Center for Economic and Civic Opinion poll. When asked how much they would support a power plant in their neighborhood, 66 percent of respondents said they would oppose it.

Many scientists warn that fossil fuel use creates emissions that threaten human health and cause global warming. Moreover, numerous scientists claim that fossil fuels are running out. As a result of these concerns, many nations have begun to revisit the energy sources that first powered human enterprises. In his 2006 State of the Union speech, U.S. President George W. Bush announced that since 2001 the United States has spent "$10 billion to develop cleaner, cheaper, and more reliable alternative energy sources," such as biomass and wind power. Despite Bush's positive rhetoric, many critics contend that the renewable energy sources he refers to are still as inefficient as they ever were and cannot possibly power modern economies. As Jerry Taylor and Peter Van Doren of the Cato Institute note, "The market share for non-hydro renewable energy . . . has languished between 1 and 3 percent for decades." Controversies such as this have been a constant throughout the history of humanity's search for the perfect energy source.

Greenhaven Press's Fueling the Future series explores this history. Each volume in the series traces the development of one energy source, and investigates the controversies surrounding its environmental impact and its potential to power humanity's future. The anthologies provide a variety of selections written by scientists, environmental activists, industry leaders, and government experts. Volumes also contain useful research tools, including an introductory essay providing important context, and an annotated table of contents that enables students to locate selections of interest easily. In addition, each volume includes an index, chronology, bibliography, glossary, and a Facts About section, which lists useful information about each energy source. Other features include numerous charts, graphs, and cartoons, which offer additional avenues for learning important information about the topic.

Fueling the Future volumes provide students with important resources for learning about the energy sources upon which human societies depend. Although it is easy to take energy for granted in developed nations, this series emphasizes how energy sources are also problematic. The U.S. Energy Information Administration calls energy "essential to life." Whether scientists will be able to develop the energy sources necessary to sustain modern life is the vital question explored in Greenhaven Press's Fueling the Future series.

# Introduction

The transition to a hydrogen economy, if it comes at all, won't happen soon.

—Robert Service, *Science*

The hydrogen economy is within sight. How fast we get there will depend on how committed we are to weaning ourselves off of oil and other fossil fuels.

—Jeremy Rifkin, *The Hydrogen Economy*

In 1874 British novelist Jules Verne published *The Mysterious Island*, an adventure tale in which five American Civil War prisoners are marooned on a strange, uncharted island. During one conversation between the men, Gideon Spillett, a reporter, poses the question of what would happen to U.S. commercial strength if the nation's coal supply was exhausted. An engineer, Cyrus Harding, is quick to respond. He predicts that American industry would turn to another fuel: water. "Yes, my friends," Harding states, "I believe that water will one day be employed as fuel, that hydrogen and oxygen which constitute it, used singly or together, will furnish an inexhaustible source of heat and light, of an intensity of which coal is not capable. . . . Water will be the coal of the future." Verne's words were visionary, especially considering that the science of his day offered only the remotest possibility of realizing such a future.

Verne's statements encouraged others to dream of a future in which heavily polluting fossil fuels such as coal would be replaced by "clean" fuels such as hydrogen. Indeed, many experts believe that the need to transition to clean fuels has become increasingly urgent as warnings about the dire consequences of global warming have increased. Moreover, countries such as the United States feel increasing pressure to cut their dependence on foreign oil. As world energy demands increase, there is less oil to go around, and each nation becomes more vulnerable to supply disruptions. Although these worries are particularly acute today, they actually began to take hold in the 1970s.

## Why the Transition to Hydrogen Has Not Yet Occurred

Such worries led to increased interest in Verne's concept of a world powered by hydrogen fuel. During this period, oil prices rose rapidly, and a worldwide environmental movement arose in response to growing concerns over pollution and global warming. One man who hypothesized about confronting these challenges was an Australian electrochemist named John Bockris. In 1975 Bockris published *Energy: The Solar-Hydrogen Alternative,* in which he detailed how hydrogen could become the primary world fuel source. He thought hydrogen could replace gasoline and thus significantly reduce the amount of

*As cars lined up to receive rationed gasoline during the gas crisis of the 1970s, many drivers began to realize that fossil fuels would not last forever.*

carbon-based pollution generated worldwide. Bockris mentioned in his book that he had previously coined the term *hydrogen economy* to describe a future in which the dirty fossil fuels that run the world's economy were replaced by efficient, nonpolluting hydrogen. The term has been used ever since, but the hydrogen economy remains an elusive goal.

The transition to a hydrogen economy has not yet taken place because all the methods available to produce usable hydrogen have serious drawbacks. Usable hydrogen is easily obtained through the process of electrolysis—the splitting of water into oxygen and hydrogen gases—but some form of energy much be expended in order to initiate the process. Fossil fuels—such as coal and natural gas—have been used to power

## The World's Leading Oil Users

| | |
|---|---|
| United States | 20.7 million |
| China | 6.5 million |
| Japan | 5.4 million |
| Germany | 2.6 million |
| Russia | 2.6 million |

Amount of Oil Used Each Day (in millions of barrels)

Source: Energy Information Administration, www.eia.doe.gov, 2004.

*An Audi hybrid is displayed at a 2006 convention of the National Hydrogen Association (NHA). The NHA supports hydrogen as an alternative energy source.*

electrolysis, but these fuels pollute. Another, more common method of producing usable hydrogen is through steam reformation—a process that uses heat to separate hydrogen from carbon-based fuels. Steam reformation is relatively inexpensive, but it still requires a fossil fuel to feed the reaction. The most environmentally friendly methods of producing hydrogen use renewable energy sources—such as solar or wind power—to drive electrolysis. These methods, however promising, are still hampered by the intermittent nature of wind power and the low energy output of solar power.

The costs of generating hydrogen through these processes also create a barrier to bringing about a hydrogen economy. If hydrogen is to be the energy that powers the economy, then it will have to be less expensive to produce than the energy derived from coal, oil, or natural gas. The U.S. Department of Energy maintains that it presently costs about $5 to generate from hydrogen the same amount of energy that is contained in one gallon of gasoline. Although gasoline prices fluctuate, Americans have never paid that much for gas. Skeptics claim that few people would embrace hydrogen as an energy source if doing so would double what they pay for energy. Supporters of a hydrogen future, however, assert that the dwindling supply of fossil fuels coupled with the environmental benefits of hydrogen fuel will compel its widespread use. The most optimistic predict that ever-improving methods of producing hydrogen will eventually lower the cost of hydrogen fuel.

## First Steps to Realizing a Hydrogen Economy

Whatever obstacles stand in the way of reaching Jules Verne's Utopia, many governments have already taken steps toward a hydrogen economy. Much of the effort is aimed at revamping the world's auto industries—developing clean, hydrogen-powered vehicles to replace gasoline- and diesel-powered vehi-

*Japan's experiments with fuel-cell powered buses underscore the nation's commitment to overcoming its dependence on polluting fossil fuels.*

*President George W. Bush is an outspoken proponent of fuel-cell technology to help reduce America's dependence on imported oil.*

cles. In the United States President George W. Bush pledged his administration's support for the development of a practical hydrogen-powered car to reduce America's dependence on foreign oil. In response, the Department of Energy organized the FreedomCAR initiative in 2002 to fund research and development on hydrogen-powered vehicles. Scientists working on the project hope to make the vehicles competitive with gasoline vehicles by 2010. Some test cities such as Los Angeles have already put hydrogen fuel cell vehicles on the road to gauge their practicality. In the European Union several nations—including Germany, Italy, the Netherlands, and Spain—have begun experimenting with hydrogen-fueled vehicles in their public transportation fleets. Similarly, Japan, which has one of the most advanced programs, has put more than forty-eight fuel cell vehicles into operation. It has also constructed ten hydrogen fueling stations around Tokyo, the nation's capital. Despite such efforts, the high cost and environmental problems associated with producing usable hydrogen remain.

Such progressive efforts, however, do reveal that expectations of a coming hydrogen economy are running high. The Department of Energy's *Hydrogen Posture Plan* of 2004, for example, foresees the transition. It states:

> In the long-term vision of the hydrogen economy (which will take several decades to achieve), hydrogen will be available in all regions of the country and will serve all sectors of the economy. It will be produced from fossil fuels [with zero pollution methods], renewable energy, and nuclear energy. It will be used throughout the transportation, electric power, and consumer sectors.

Skeptics are not so confident, noting that predictions about the coming of a hydrogen economy have been made since the 1970s. Meanwhile, scientists have yet to solve the economic and environmental problems that have plagued hydrogen technology. Some even fear that focusing on hoped-for breakthroughs that would enable a hydrogen economy undercuts the development of other energy sources, such as solar and wind power, that have more promise, at least in the short term.

The emphasis on speeding the development of a hydrogen economy remains the subject of intense debate. To be sure, whether hydrogen will be the solution to the energy needs of the twenty-first century remains to be seen. The hydrogen economy may be close at hand or always just out of reach; only time will tell if technology, circumstance, and the will of the world's people can make Jules Verne's vision a reality.

# CHAPTER 1

# Developing Hydrogen as an Energy Carrier

# Pioneers in Hydrogen Energy

## Peter Hoffmann

In the following article journalist Peter Hoffmann describes scientists' early attempts to develop hydrogen as a practical energy source. He begins with the Reverend William Cecil, who argued for replacing early nineteenth-century steam engines with engines run on hydrogen gas. Hoffmann then describes the experiments of various other scientists who believed that the highly flammable gas was a useful yet untapped fuel. Hoffmann next explores the work of German engineer Rudolf Erren, who developed practical applications for hydrogen fuel during the 1930s and 1940s. Erren's engines (which were made to run on hydrogen or a mix of hydrogen and other combustible gases) powered buses, submarines, and other machinery. His engines proved that hydrogen could be used as an alternative to coal and oil. Hoffmann concludes by discussing how engineers eventually built the first practical hydrogen fuel cell in the 1950s. This portable storage technology gave many scientists hope that hydrogen energy could make the world less dependent on dirty and exhaustible fossil fuels. Peter Hoffmann is editor and publisher of *The Hydrogen & Fuel Cell Letter*, an alternative energy periodical. He is a former Washington correspondent for McGraw-Hill World News.

On November 27, 1820, the dons of Cambridge University assembled to hear a clergyman's proposal. It is recorded in the transactions of the Cambridge Philosophical Society that Rev. W. Cecil, M.A., Fellow of Magdalen College and of the society,

Peter Hoffmann, *Tomorrow's Energy: Hydrogen, Fuel Cells, and the Prospects for a Cleaner Planet*. Cambridge, MA: The MIT Press, 2001. Copyright © 2001. Reproduced by permission of The MIT Press, Cambridge, MA.

read a lengthy treatise, titled On the Application of Hydrogen Gas to Produce Moving Power in Machinery, describing an engine operated by the "Pressure of the Atmosphere upon a Vacuum Caused by Explosions of Hydrogen Gas and Atmospheric Air." Cecil first dwelt on the disadvantages of water-driven engines (which could be used only "where water is abundant") and steam engines (which were slow in getting underway). The utility of a steam engine was "much diminished by the tedious and laborious preparation which is necessary to bring it into action." Furthermore, "a small steam engine not exceeding the power of one man cannot be brought into action in less than half an hour: and a four-horse steam engine cannot be used [without] two hours preparation." A hydrogen-powered engine would solve these problems, Cecil averred: "The engine in which hydrogen gas is employed to produce moving force was intended to unite two principal advantages of water and steam so as to be capable of acting in any place without the delay and labour of preparation." Rather prophetically, Cecil added: "It may be inferior, in some respects, to many engines at present employed; yet it will not be wholly useless, if, together with its own defects, it should be found to possess advantages also peculiar to itself."

## From Principles to Practical Concepts

According to Cecil's explanations, the general principle was that hydrogen, when mixed with air and ignited, would produce a large partial vacuum. The air rushing back into the vacuum after the explosion could be harnessed as a moving force "nearly in the same manner as in the common steam engine: the difference consists chiefly in the manner of forming the vacuum. . . . If two and a half measures by bulk of atmospheric air be mixed with one measure of hydrogen, and a flame be applied, the mixed gas will expand into a space rather greater than three times its original bulk."

Cecil went on to discuss the workings of his engine in considerable detail. The Transactions of the Cambridge Philosophical Society did not record whether Cecil actually ever built such an engine. In any event, Cecil's proposal was the first known instance of an early technologist's attempting to put the special qualities of hydrogen to work.

# How a Fuel Cell Operates

When hydrogen and oxygen are forced together within the cell, electricity is produced. By-products include heat and water.

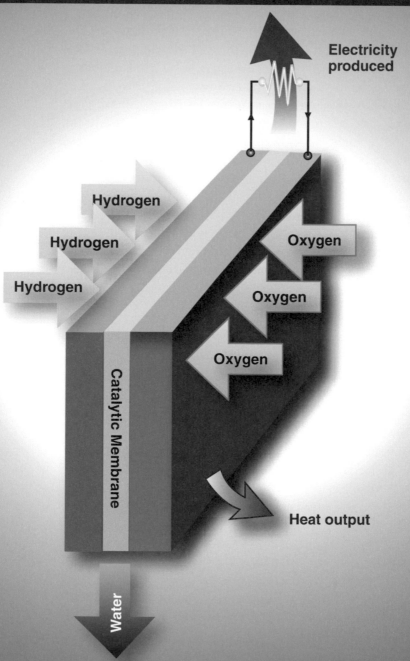

Electricity produced

Hydrogen

Hydrogen

Hydrogen

Oxygen

Oxygen

Oxygen

Catalytic Membrane

Heat output

Water

Cecil's suggestion came only 20 years after another fundamental discovery: electrolysis (breaking water down into hydrogen and oxygen by passing an electrical current through it). That discovery had been made by two English scientists, William Nicholson and Sir Anthony Carlisle, 6 years after [the eighteenth-century French chemist who named hydrogen, Antoine Laurent] Lavoisier's execution [in 1794, during the French Revolution] and just a few weeks after the Italian physicist Alessandro Volta built his first electric cell.

In the next 150 years or so hydrogen's unique properties were discussed with increasing frequency by scientists and by writers of early science fiction. . . .

The 1920s and the 1930s witnessed a flowering of interest, especially in Germany and England but also in Canada, in hydrogen as fuel. The evolution of Canada's Electrolyser Corporation Ltd.—today one of the world's leading makers of electrolytic hydrogen plants (it has delivered some 900 systems to 91 countries)—began early in the twentieth century. Around 1905 Alexander T. Stuart, the father of the current chairman,

*Although he did not discover hydrogen, Antoine Laurent Lavoisier gave the element its name from the Greek words for "born of water."*

Alexander K. "Sandy" Stuart, began to take an interest in hydrogen energy while studying chemistry and mineralogy at the University of Toronto. Young Stuart and one of his professors, Lash Miller (a former student of the fuel cell's inventor, William Grove), had noted that most of Canada was importing almost all its fuel except for wood. "At the same time, Niagara Falls' hydroelectric generating capacity was being utilized at a capacity factor of only 30–40 percent," Sandy Stuart related in 1996 in the first of a series of lectures bearing his name at the University of Sherbrooke. "The question was, how could such surplus capacity be converted to fuel energy? The obvious answer was electrolysis of water. This led to our first experimental electrolysers."

As it turned out, Stuart electrolysers came into commercial use not to make hydrogen fuel but to make hydrogen and oxygen for the purpose of cutting steel. The first electrolysers were shipped in 1920 to what was then the Stuart Oxygen Company in San Francisco. Four years later, the Canadian government began supporting the use of Stuart electrolysis cells to make fertilizer in British Columbia. From the mid 1920s on, the elder Stuart also developed concepts for the Ontario Hydro utility to integrate hydroelectric energy with coal, coke, or other carbon sources to make "town gas" (carbon monoxide and hydrogen) for domestic heating, to produce a range of synthetic chemicals (including methanol), and to directly reduce iron ore to iron. In 1934 Ontario Hydro built a 400-kilowatt electrolysis plant, and there were plans to heat buildings with hydrogen and even to run test vehicles on it, but that project was terminated after 2 years. All these efforts ended with changes in Ontario's governments, but mostly with Canada's entry into World War II and with the arrival of natural gas on Canada's energy scene after the war.

## Early Applications

On the conceptual level, one of the most important figures in those early years was John Burdon Sanderson Haldane, a physiologist turned geneticist, longtime editorial board director of the communist newspaper *The Daily Worker,* and in the 1960s an émigré to India and a guru to that country's growing science establishment. In 1923, when he was only in his late twenties, Haldane gave a famous lecture at Cambridge University in which he said that hydrogen—derived from wind power via electrolysis, liquefied, and stored—would be the fuel of the future. . . .

Also in Britain, Harry Ricardo (one of the pioneers in the development of the internal-combustion engine) and A.F. Burstall were among the first to investigate the burn characteristics of hydrogen, and W. Hastings Campbell, the German Rudolf Erren (who spent most of the 1930s in England), and R. O. King (then with the British Air Ministry Laboratory) worked on hydrogen as a fuel.

In Germany, Franz Lawaczeck, Rudolf Erren, Kurt Weil, J.E. Noeggerath, Hermann Honnef, and other engineers and inven-

*For centuries, water has been harnessed for power. Niagara Falls on the U.S.-Canadian border has several hydroelectric power stations along its length.*

tors were researching hydrogen and advocating its use as a fuel. . . . Lawaczeck, a turbine designer, became interested in hydrogen as early as 1907. By 1919 he was sketching concepts for hydrogen-powered cars, trains, and engines. Some of his inspiration came from contact with his cousin J.E. Noeggerath, an American of German birth who worked in Schenectady, New York, and later in Berlin. Lawaczeck and Noeggerath collaborated in developing an efficient pressurized electrolyzer. In the 1930s, Lawaczeck was apparently the first to suggest that energy could be transported via hydrogen-carrying pipelines. Honnef dreamed of huge steel towers, up to 750 feet in height, each with as many as five 480-foot windmills producing up to 100 megawatts each, which would be stored in the form of hydrogen; however, his concepts were never developed beyond the construction of a 50-meter prototype tower.

*The German dirigible* Hindenburg *glides above New York City in 1936. The explosion of the airship in 1937 was wrongly blamed on the hydrogen inside it.*

In Italy, a 1937 article in the journal *Rivista Aeronautica* mentioned in passing the experimental efforts of the engineer A. Beldimano to adapt liquid hydrogen for use in aircraft engines. . . .

One of the earliest and most fascinating efforts involving hydrogen was its use as not only a buoyancy medium but also a booster fuel for the Zeppelins, the huge German dirigibles that provided leisurely and elegant transatlantic air travel in the 1920s and the 1930s. Normally, these big skyships carried large amounts of liquid fuel (usually a benzol-gasoline mixture) that was used to drive 12- or 16-cylinder engines, which typically propelled a Zeppelin at an altitude of 2400 feet and a speed of not quite 75 miles per hour—provided there was no headwind. Fuel economy was one problem for the Zeppelin; another was how to reduce buoyancy as fuel consumption reduced a ship's weight. According to a 1929 report by the Zeppelin Company, the rule of thumb was that a Zeppelin's captain had to blow off about a cubic meter of hydrogen for every kilogram of fuel burned up during a nonstop cruise, which typically lasted 3–5 days. Better fuel economy could be achieved by certain engine modifications, such as increasing the compression ratios, but the buoyancy problem persisted. The solution was as simple as it was ingenious: Why not burn the blow-off hydrogen as extra fuel together with the main fuel supply? Zeppelin's engineers found that this was feasible. The addition of between 5 percent and 30 percent hydrogen to the main fuel at compression ratios as high as 10:1 produced substantially higher power output—as much as 325 brake horsepower, in comparison with the normal 269 bhp. It also achieved substantial energy savings. The test-bed findings were confirmed by an 82-hour, 6000-mile cruise over the Mediterranean Sea in 1928, during which a fuel reduction of about 14 percent was achieved. . . .

## Erren's Engines

One of the best-known hydrogen advocates of the 1930s and the 1940s was Rudolf Erren, a brilliant, visionary German engineer who had trucks, buses, submarines, and internal-combustion engines of all kinds running on hydrogen and other fuels, conventional and unconventional. Erren engines were powering vehicles in sizable numbers in Germany and in England. A flinty engineer from Upper Silesia (now part of Poland) with a pronounced disdain for academics and theoreticians, Erren formed his first company, Erren Motoren GmbH Spezialversuchsanstalt, in a grimy industrial section of northern Berlin in 1928. Two years earlier, he had begun to investigate hydrogen and its properties, pursuing an interest that went back to his childhood. When I visited him in Hannover in 1976, he told me that he . . . had read [Max] Pemberton's *Iron Pirate* as a child. As he recalled the book, it "described a pirate group that had kidnapped a German professor who had developed a hydrogen engine which made the pirates' ship much faster than other ships."

Erren had experimented with hydrogen while attending high school in Katowice. His interest in hydrogen carried over as a hobby through his university years in Berlin, in Göttingen, and in England. "During summer vacations when other students went on vacation," he recalled, "I worked in engine workshops to learn something because I wanted to know these things in practice. Theory alone doesn't work." In 1928 he won his first patents, one of them for a hydrogen engine. Erren presented his data at the 1930 World Power Conference in Berlin. According to him, the terms "Erren Engine," "Erren Process," and "Erren System," now largely forgotten, were then officially recognized to differentiate his combustion process from any other.

In 1930, at the invitation of several British firms, Erren went to London to found the Erren Engineering Company. There he continued his work on developing advanced combustion processes that would permit hydrogen to be used alone as a fuel or as a "clean-up" additive to normal fuels. The technique of "Errenizing" any type of internal-combustion process was apparently relatively well known in the 1930s, at least among automotive engineers. Essentially it meant injecting slightly pressurized hydrogen into air or oxygen inside the combustion chamber, rather than feeding the air-fuel mixture via a carburetor into the engine, a method that commonly resulted in violent backfiring. Erren's patented system required special fuel injection and control mechanisms but left the other engine components intact. With hydrogen used as a booster, the Erren system eliminated backfiring and achieved much better combustion of hydrocarbons with higher output and lower specific fuel consumption. . . .

## Hints of a Coming Hydrogen Economy

Interest in hydrogen picked up again around 1950 in the context of fuel cells. Francis T. Bacon, a British scientist, developed the first practical hydrogen-air fuel cell (a development that was to be of great significance later in the American space program).

Also in the 1950s, a German physicist was becoming interested in hydrogen as an energy-storage medium. Eduard Justi, a

*Francis T. Bacon stands beside his hydrogen fuel cell in 1959. Bacon demonstrated his first 5-kilowatt cell by using it to power a welding machine.*

distinguished German electrochemist at the University of Braunschweig, had been working for years on the development of new, more efficient fuel cells. In a 1962 monograph titled *Cold Combustion—Fuel Cells*, Eduard Justi and a co-worker, August Winsel, discussed the prospects of splitting water into hydrogen and oxygen, storing these gases separately, and recombining them in fuel cells. Justi later amplified his ideas in the 1965 book *Energieumwandlung in Festkörpern*, in which he proposed using solar energy to produce hydrogen along the Mediterranean and piping it to Germany and other countries.

In 1962, John Bockris, an Australian electrochemist, proposed a plan to supply US cities with solar-derived energy via hydrogen. Bockris (who in 1975 published *Energy: The Solar-Hydrogen Alternative*, the first detailed overview of a future solar-hydrogen economy), says that the term "hydrogen economy"—which has multiple economic and environmental meanings—was coined in 1970 during a discussion at the General Motors Technical Center in Warren, Michigan. Bockris, at the time a consultant to GM, was discussing prospects for other fuels to replace gasoline and thereby help to eliminate pollution, a subject that was then beginning to creep into the public consciousness.

# A Visionary Predicts the Broad Use of Hydrogen Energy

## J.B.S. Haldane

John Burdon Sanderson Haldane was a British sociologist, geneticist, and evolutionary biologist. At England's Cambridge University in 1923, while he was still in his twenties, Haldane gave a lecture that was noted for its accuracy in predicting technologies that would impact society in the future. The paper, which was later printed in book form, contained a short section on Haldane's predictions for the future production of energy. Reprinted in the following selection, Haldane's forecasts centered on a belief that the depletion of Britain's coal and oil resources would force the nation to embrace alternative energies within four hundred years. Haldane predicted that wind power would dominate in the twenty-fourth century. That power, Haldane writes, would be used in the electrolysis of water to fill storage tanks with hydrogen and oxygen gases. These gases could then be used in combustion engines or to power fuel cells. His statements have inspired scientists and engineers who believe that hydrogen energy will be the most important energy source in the future.

As for the supplies of mechanical power, it is axiomatic that the exhaustion of our coal and oil-fields is a matter of centuries only. As it has often been assumed that their exhaustion would lead to the collapse of industrial civilization,

I may perhaps be pardoned if I give some of the reasons which lead me to doubt this proposition.

Water-power is not, I think, a probable substitute, on account of its small quantity, seasonal fluctuation, and sporadic distribution. It may perhaps, however, shift the centre of industrial gravity to well-watered mountainous tracts such as the Himalayan foothills, British Columbia, and Armenia. Ultimately we shall have to tap those intermittent but inexhaustible sources of power, the wind and the sunlight. The problem is simply one of storing their energy in a form as convenient as coal or petrol [gasoline]. If a windmill in one's back garden could produce a hundredweight of coal daily (and it can produce its equivalent in energy), our coal-mines would shut down to-morrow. Even to-morrow a cheap, fool-proof, and durable storage battery may be invented, which will enable us to transform the intermittent energy of the wind into continuous electric power.

*In 1923 British sociologist J.B.S. Haldane predicted that future energy needs would be met by wind power.*

## Stored Gases and Fuel Cells

Personally, I think that four hundred years hence the power question in England may be solved somewhat as follows: The country will be covered with rows of metallic windmills working electric motors which in their turn supply current at a very high voltage to great electric mains. At suitable distances, there will be great power-stations where during windy weather the surplus power will be used for the electrolytic decomposition of water into oxygen and hydrogen. These gases will be liquefied, and stored in vats, vacuum-jacketed reservoirs, probably sunk in the ground. If these reservoirs are sufficiently large, the loss of liquid due to leakage

# How Wind Can Be Used to Make Hydrogen Fuel

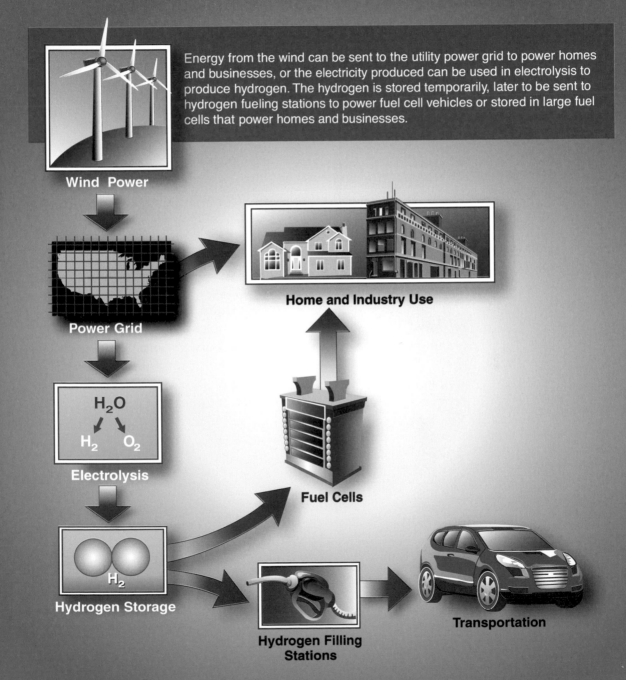

Energy from the wind can be sent to the utility power grid to power homes and businesses, or the electricity produced can be used in electrolysis to produce hydrogen. The hydrogen is stored temporarily, later to be sent to hydrogen fueling stations to power fuel cell vehicles or stored in large fuel cells that power homes and businesses.

**Wind Power**

**Power Grid**

$H_2O$

$H_2$   $O_2$

**Electrolysis**

$H_2$

**Hydrogen Storage**

**Home and Industry Use**

**Fuel Cells**

**Hydrogen Filling Stations**

**Transportation**

Source: Nordic H$_2$ Energy Foresight, www.h2foresight.info, 2005.

inwards of heat will not be great; thus the proportion evaporating daily from a reservoir 100 yards square by 60 feet deep would not be $\frac{1}{1000}$; of that lost from a tank measuring two feet each way. In times of calm, the gases will be recombined in explosion-motors working dynamos which produce electrical energy once more, or more probably in oxidation cells. Liquid hydrogen is weight for weight the most efficient known method of storing energy, as it gives about three times as much heat per pound as petrol. On the other hand, it is very light, and bulk for bulk has only one-third of the efficiency of petrol. This will not, however, detract from its use in aeroplanes, where weight is more important than bulk. These huge reservoirs of liquefied gases will enable wind-energy to be stored, so that it can be expended for industry, transportation, heating, and lighting, as desired. The initial costs will be very considerable, but the running expenses less than those of our present system. Among its more obvious advantages will be the fact that energy will be as cheap in one part of the country as another, so that industry will be greatly decentralized; and that no smoke or ash will be produced.

It is on some such lines as these, I think, that the problem will be solved. It is essentially a practical problem, and the exhaustion of our coal-fields will furnish the necessary stimulus for its solution. . . . I may add in parenthesis that, on thermodynamical grounds which I can hardly summarize shortly, I do not much believe in the commercial possibility of induced radio-activity.

# How Hydrogen Fuel Is Currently Produced

## International Energy Agency

The International Energy Agency (IEA) was established in 1974 to develop and implement international energy policies. The organization is a collective of thirty member countries, including the United States, Canada, Turkey, South Korea, and several European nations. In the following selection the IEA describes several methods currently used to obtain hydrogen fuel. The majority of these methods use electrolysis to split water into hydrogen and oxygen atoms. Some of the processes collect the water created when carbon-based fuels mix with steam during electrolysis. This method, however, produces carbon dioxide (a greenhouse gas) as a by-product, making the method less appealing because of its potential harm to the environment. Other processes that apply electrolysis to water require the use of fossil-fuel energy to split the water molecules. These processes are environmentally unfriendly as well. Scientists are thus investigating still other methods that use renewable energy sources to drive electrolysis. These methods produce no harmful by-products but are costly and inefficient. As the IEA points out, none of the technologies presently in use are clean, efficient, and cost-effective. Thus, further research and development are needed to make hydrogen a viable energy source.

While advancements in fuel cell technology tend to grab the headlines, a critical hurdle blocking the road toward a viable "hydrogen economy" is the efficient, cost-effective and clean production of hydrogen. . . .

International Energy Agency, *Hydrogen & Fuel Cells: Review of National R&D Programs.* Paris: Organisation for Economic Co-operation and Development/International Energy Agency, 2004. Reproduced by permission.

Researchers are developing a wide range of processes for producing hydrogen economically and in an environmentally friendly way. Most methods of producing hydrogen involve electrolysis—or splitting water ($H_2O$) into its component parts of hydrogen ($H_2$) and oxygen (O). The most common process is currently steam reforming of natural gas, which converts methane (and other hydrocarbons in natural gas) into hydrogen and carbon monoxide by reaction with steam over a nickel catalyst. Other methods include:

- High-temperature steam electrolysis uses heat (approximately 1000°C) to provide some of the energy needed to split water, making the process more energy efficient.
- Thermo-chemical water splitting uses chemicals and heat in multiple steps to split water into its component parts.
- Photo-electrochemical systems use semi-conducting materials (like photovoltaics) to split water using only sunlight.
- Photo-biological systems use micro-organisms to split water using sunlight.
- Biological systems use microbes to break down a variety of biomass feedstocks into hydrogen.
- Gasification using heat to break down biomass or coal into a gas from which pure hydrogen can be generated.

## Electrolysis

Notably, electrolysis opens the door to producing hydrogen from any energy source capable of generating electricity, including fossil fuels, nuclear and renewable energies, such as solar, wind, or hydropower. But electrolysis requires substantial amounts of electricity, and is ultimately only as environmentally-friendly as the energy source used to generate the electricity. In terms of the ideal "hydrogen economy", it is anticipated that the electricity required for the electrolysis process would come from renewable sources—because the production of hydrogen fuel that increases demand for fossil fuels promises no greenhouse gas mitigation (under current scenarios and absent effective $CO_2$ [carbon dioxide] capture and storage). Currently, electrolysis provides only a small percentage of the world's hydrogen, most of which is

# How Electrolysis Is Used to Produce Hydrogen

This diagram shows a container of water into which two electrodes have been immersed. As an electrical current is passed through the water, the ions in the water separate. The positively charged ions move to the cathode while the negatively charged ions move to the anode. At the ends of each electrode, electrons are absorbed or released by the ions, producing oxygen gas. At the cathode, electrons are absorbed by the ions, producing hydrogen gas.

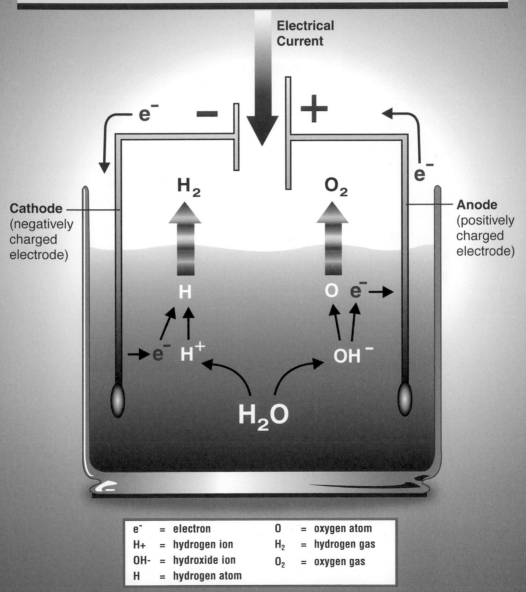

Electrical Current

e⁻  −     +  e⁻

H₂          O₂

Cathode (negatively charged electrode)

Anode (positively charged electrode)

H          O  e⁻ →

→ e⁻ H⁺          OH⁻

H₂O

| e⁻ | = electron | O | = oxygen atom |
| H+ | = hydrogen ion | H₂ | = hydrogen gas |
| OH- | = hydroxide ion | O₂ | = oxygen gas |
| H | = hydrogen atom | | |

Source: New Mexico Solar Energy Association, "Electrolysis: Obtaining Hydrogen from Water: The Basis for a Solar-Hydrogen Economy," www.nmsea.org.

supplied to industrial applications requiring small volumes of high purity hydrogen. Finally, it is expected that it will be decades before improvements in renewable energy technologies would yield electricity at a price which would enable hydrogen to compete with conventional forms of energy. . . .

## Hydrogen from Fossil Fuels

Hydrogen gas can be derived from hydrogen-rich fossil fuels through a variety of processes. Currently, the most prevalent and least-expensive way to produce hydrogen is to derive it from natural gas through a process called steam reformation. Hydrogen can also

*This coal gasification plant in Louisiana heats coal until it gasifies. The products of the combustion process include hydrogen and syngas, a carbon-based fuel.*

be "harvested" from coal, through gasification. Fossil fuels can indirectly be used to produce hydrogen when they are used to generate electricity used in the electrolysis of water. Since this practice includes emissions related to the fossil fuel consumption, hydrogen R&D [research and development] programs involving electrolysis from fossil energy sources tend to include work on methods to reduce these emissions, such as carbon capture and storage. The current [2004] hydrogen world production rounds to some 40 million tons a year. Most of this hydrogen is produced from steam reforming of natural gas and used in refinery as a process gas, in chemical industry and in metal manufacturing.

## Steam Reformation

Steam reforming uses thermal energy to separate hydrogen from the carbon component of hydrogen-rich fuels by reacting them with steam on catalytic surfaces. Although steam reformation is a relatively efficient and inexpensive process, this depends upon the fluctuating price of natural gas (or other feedstock fuel). In terms of the environment, steam reformation generates $CO_2$ emissions, both as a by-product of the reformation process and during fossil fuel production and transportation (upstream) phases. . . .

## Gasification of Coal

Gasification of coal may be the oldest method of producing hydrogen. This technique was the source of the "city gas" that was originally supplied to many cities in Europe and Australia before natural gas became available. This gas contains up to 60% hydrogen, but also large amounts of CO [carbon monoxide]. To make it, the coal is typically heated to 900°C where it turns into a gaseous form; it is then mixed with steam and in the presence of a catalyst a mixture of $H_2$, CO and $CO_2$ is produced. In addition, sulphur and nitrogen compounds are released during the process, which like the CO and $CO_2$, must be handled in an environmentally-friendly way. . . .

*Although wind turbines produce energy without generating pollution, the wind is an unreliable energy source because it does not blow consistently.*

## Hydrogen from Renewable Sources

The idea of a hydrogen economy based on renewable energy sources is continuously gaining importance, largely due to increasing concern regarding growth of energy demand, global warming and security of fuel supply. For these reasons, and in the long-term, renewable energy sources are expected to provide the energy to produce hydrogen. For this to happen, large scale renewable energy production is an essential precondition for the credible deployment of a sustainable hydrogen economy. In the meantime, hydrogen technologies may help increase the penetration of renewables as back-up power for intermittent energy sources. . . . Electrolysis technologies will clearly be an important element of the cost efficiency of using renewable energy to produce hydrogen. . . .

## Wind

A good example of R&D into the potential of renewable hydrogen production is the . . . Utsira demonstration project sponsored by the Norwegian government. The project is evaluating the sustainability of using a wind turbine to generate electricity feeding an electrolyser for producing hydrogen, which in turn will be used in PEM [proton exchange membrane] fuel cells. In Sweden a hydrogen filling station went in operation in Malmö in September 2003. The hydrogen production is from electrolysis of water using electricity from wind power bought by contract from the grid. The hydrogen may ultimately be used directly to fuel hydrogen fuel cell vehicles at the station, but the first step is to mix the hydrogen with natural gas for use in buses in Malmö. The Australian government and the University of Tasmania constructed two large wind turbines at Mawson Base in Antarctica with the objective to supply the base's annual electricity requirements and to produce sufficient hydrogen for use as transport fuel.[1]

## Solar

In Australia, research is under way on solar electrolysis applications for both the public and private sectors. With respect to solar-based hydrogen production, Canada is developing photovoltaic electrolyser-fuel cell technologies, including storage capabilities.[2] . . . In Canada, the National Research Council in Vancouver is also demonstrating the combination of hydrogen PEM fuel cells with photovoltaic and electrolyser powering systems as a back-up power for buildings.

---

1. Similar experiments are being conducted in Spain, Greece, Germany, and Portugal.
2. Other nations are also investigating photovoltaic storage systems.

Researchers are also demonstrating that highly concentrated sunlight can be used to generate the high temperatures needed to split water or methane into hydrogen and carbon. Concentrated solar energy can also be used to generate temperatures of several hundred to over 2,000 degrees at which thermochemical reaction cycles can be used to produce hydrogen. Such high-temperature, high-flux solar driven thermochemical processes offer a novel approach for the environmentally benign production of hydrogen. Very high reaction rates at these elevated temperatures enhance the production rates significantly and more than compensate for the intermittent nature of the solar resource. . . .

### Hydro
In Switzerland, hydrogen production work focuses on high pressure electrolysis of water, deriving from the extensively available hydropower plants. . . .

## Hydrogen from Biomass
Thermochemical processes can also be applied to bioresources such as agricultural residues and wastes or biomass specifically grown as an energy crop to produce hydrogen through pyrolysis and gasification.[3] This process generates a carbon-rich synthetic gas that can be reformed into hydrogen using thermal processing techniques similar to fossil fuels reformation.

Gasification technology has been under intensive development over the last two decades; a number of demonstration facilities have been tested and many units are in operation. Until recently, biomass gasification has been employed to produce electricity or heat—which has rarely justified the capital and operating costs. But the increasing demand for hydrogen is driving research and development of biomass gasification projects. . . .

3. A combination of processes that degrade waste by heating to ash and then converting residual hydrocarbons to gas.

# Hydrogen Production from Nuclear Energy

Hydrogen production holds renewed promise for nuclear energy, as nuclear-based hydrogen production can provide an essentially carbon emissions–free source of hydrogen, significantly reduce dependence on fossil fuels, and open a new area of application for nuclear energy that may eventually exceed the use of nuclear power for electricity.

Three approaches are being investigated: The first is to use nuclear heat to assist with the energy needs required by steam reformation for producing hydrogen from fossil fuels (e.g., natural gas). Secondly, several direct thermochemical processes are being developed for producing hydrogen from water. For economic production, high temperatures are required to ensure rapid throughput and high conversion efficiencies. A third way, of course, is to use nuclear power to supply electricity for electrolysis.

Production of hydrogen via high-temperature steam electrolysis has the potential for much higher overall efficiency than room-temperature electrolysis. In particular, high-temperature electrolytic water-splitting supported by nuclear process heat and electricity has the potential to produce hydrogen with an overall system efficiency near those of the hydrocarbon and the thermochemical processes, but without the corrosive conditions of thermochemical processes, the fossil fuel consumption and greenhouse gas emissions associated with hydrocarbon processes. . . .

## Photo-Electrochemical

Photo-electrochemical (PEC) processes can produce hydrogen in one step—

## FACTS TO CONSIDER

### Scientists Are Exploring New Ways to Make Hydrogen

Electrolysis makes hydrogen by splitting a water molecule with electricity. The electricity could come from solar cells, windmills, hydropower or safer, next-generation nuclear reactors. Researchers are also trying to use microbes to transform biomass, including parts of crops that now have no economic value, into hydrogen. In [2004] researchers at the University of Minnesota and the University of Patras in Greece announced a chemical reactor that generates hydrogen from ethanol mixed with water. Though appealing, all these technologies are either unaffordable or unavailable on a commercial scale and are likely to remain so for many years to come.

Matthew L. Wald, *Scientific American*, May 2004.

splitting water by illuminating a water-immersed semiconductor with sunlight. There are two types of photo-electrochemical processes. The first uses soluble metal complexes as catalysts. When these complexes dissolve, they absorb solar energy and produce an electrical charge that drives the water splitting reaction. This process mimics photo-synthesis: however, currently there is minimal experience in this process.

The second method uses semiconducting electrodes in a photochemical cell to convert light energy into chemical energy. The semiconductor surface serves two functions, to absorb solar energy and to act as an electrode. However, light-induced corrosion limits the useful life of the semiconductor.

*Within this transparent apparatus is a semiconductor immersed in water. The semiconductor catches solar energy and uses it to split the water to make hydrogen.*

The key challenges to advance PEC cell innovation toward the market concern the progress needed in material science and engineering. The development of highly efficient corrosion-resistant photoelectrode materials and their processing technologies are most important. Since no "ideal" photoelectrode material for water splitting exists, commercially, new materials have to be engineered and synthesised. . . .

## Biological and Photolytic Systems

Recently, increased attention has been focused on photolytic and biological means of hydrogen production—for example, solar thermal processes, photo-electrolysis, photo-catalytic and photo-biological processes. Biological production of hydrogen using micro-algal photo-synthesis is a process whereby hydrogen is derived from organic matter and water by micro-organisms such as algae and cyano-bacteria. The most common examples of organic feedstock include biomass crops, agricultural as well as animal wastes, and soils. The natural micro-algal hydrogen metabolism has to be genetically engineered in order to achieve significant, "natural overproduction" of hydrogen.

Many small-scale projects have successfully demonstrated the ability of these technologies to produce hydrogen. The R&D is still in its infancy and production costs remain significant. Nonetheless, the body of knowledge in this area of research is increasing rapidly. . . .

## Hydrogen Production from Boron

Since about 64% of world boron reserves are found in Turkey, scientific studies are being conducted in Turkey to investigate the potential of boron as a hydrogen carrying material for use in fuel cells. Turkey is planning to upgrade the utilisation of this natural source, and will invite researchers, investors and international organisations to cooperate on hydrogen energy studies.

## CHAPTER 2

# Is Hydrogen Technology Viable?

The U.S. government has given hundreds of millions of dollars in grants to automakers such as Ford that develop fuel cell vehicles.

# Hydrogen Technology Is Efficient

## Amory B. Lovins

Amory B. Lovins is an experimental physicist and the chief executive officer of the Rocky Mountain Institute, a Colorado-based nonprofit organization that is concerned with sustaining the planet's resources. In the following selection from his often quoted "Twenty Hydrogen Myths," Lovins argues that hydrogen power is efficient enough to be competitive with fossil fuels. He counters what he believes are two myths concerning hydrogen: that making it uses more energy than it yields and that the technology to run cars on hydrogen is impractical. In fact, Lovins claims, hydrogen fuel cell technology is even more efficient than combustion engines in powering vehicles. He also asserts that fuel cells may one day supply electricity to local power grids for residential and industrial use.

## Myth

*Making hydrogen uses more energy than it yields, so it's prohibitively inefficient.*

Any conversion from one form of energy to another consumes more useful energy than it yields. If it could do the opposite, creating energy out of nothing, you could create a perpetual-motion machine violating the laws of physics. Conversion losses are unavoidable; the issue is whether they're worth incurring. If they were intolerable as a matter of principle, . . . then we'd have to stop making gasoline from crude oil (~73–91% efficient from wellhead to retail pump) and electricity from fossil fuel (~29–35% efficient from coal at the power plant to retail meter). Such conversion losses are thus not specific to producing hydrogen. Hydrogen production is typically ~72–85% efficient in natural-gas reformers or ~70–75% efficient in electrolyzers; the rest is heat that may also be reusable. (These efficiency figures are all reduced by 15% because of the way hydrogen's energy content is normally measured.) So why incur these losses to make hydrogen? Because hydrogen's greater end-use efficiency can more than offset the conversion losses, much as an electric heat pump or air conditioner can offset fuel-to-electricity conversion losses by using one unit of electricity to concentrate and deliver several units of heat. That is, conversion losses and costs are tolerable if the resulting form of energy is more efficiently or conveniently usable than the original form, hence justified by its greater economic *value*. Making hydrogen can readily achieve this goal.

Crude oil can be more efficiently converted into delivered gasoline than can natural gas into delivered hydrogen. But that's a red herring: the difference is far more than offset by the hydrogen's 2–3-fold higher efficiency in running a fuel-cell car than gasoline's in running an engine-driven car. Using Japanese round numbers from Toyota, 88% of oil at the wellhead ends up as gasoline in your tank, and then 16% of that gasoline energy reaches the wheels of your typical modern car, so the well-to-wheels efficiency is 14%. A gasoline-fueled hybrid-electric car like the 2002 Toyota *Prius* nearly doubles the gasoline-to-wheels efficiency from 16% to 30% and the overall well-to-wheels efficiency from 14% to 26%. But locally reforming natural gas can deliver 70% of the gas's wellhead energy into the car's compressed-hydrogen tank. That "meager" conversion efficiency is then more than offset by an advanced fuel-cell drivesystem's superior 60% efficiency in converting that hydrogen energy into traction, for an overall well-to-wheels efficiency of 42%. That's three times higher than the normal gasoline-engine car's, or 1.5 times higher than the gasoline-hybrid-electric car's. This helps explain why most automakers see today's gasoline-hybrid cars as a stepping-stone to their ultimate goal—direct-hydrogen fuel-cell cars.

In competitive electricity markets, it may even make good economic sense to use hydrogen as an electricity storage medium.

True, the overall round-trip efficiency of using electricity to split water, making hydrogen, storing it, and then converting it back into electricity in a fuel cell is relatively low at about 45% (after 25% electrolyzer losses and 40% fuel-cell losses) plus any by-product heat recaptured from both units for space-conditioning or water heating. But this can still be worthwhile because it uses power from an efficient baseload plant (perhaps even a combined-cycle plant converting 50–60% of its fuel to electricity) to displace a very inefficient peaking power plant (a simple-cycle gas turbine or engine-generator, often only 15–20% efficient).

*The Toyota Prius is an efficient hybrid vehicle whose part-combustion, part-electric engine offers amazing fuel economy.*

# How Hydrogen Travels from Production to End Use

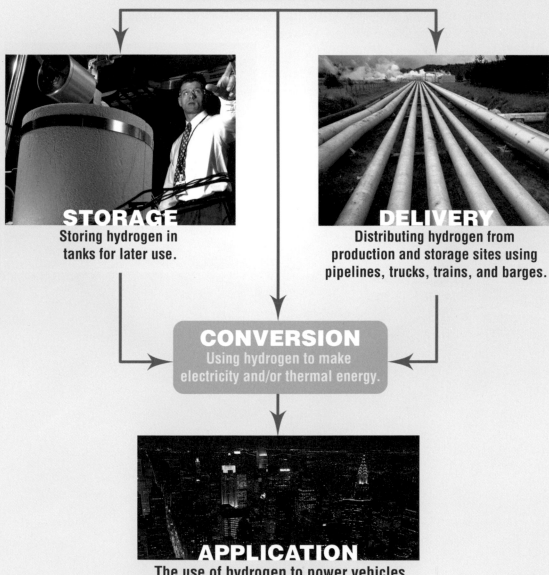

## PRODUCTION
The production of hydrogen using
fossil fuels, biomass, or water.

## STORAGE
Storing hydrogen in
tanks for later use.

## DELIVERY
Distributing hydrogen from
production and storage sites using
pipelines, trucks, trains, and barges.

## CONVERSION
Using hydrogen to make
electricity and/or thermal energy.

## APPLICATION
The use of hydrogen to power vehicles,
homes, and businesses.

Source: U.S. Department of Energy, *Hydrogen Posture Plan*, www.eere.energy.gov, 2004.

This peak-shaving value is reflected in the marketplace. When the cost of peak power for the top 50–150 hours a year is $600–900/MWh [megawatts per hour], typically 30–40 times the cost of baseload power (~$20/MWh), the economics of storage become quite interesting. Distributed generation provides not only energy and peak capacity, but also ancillary services and deferral of grid upgrades. Hydrogen storage can also save power-plant fuel by permitting more flexible operation of the utility system with fuller utilization of intermittent sources like wind. Once all the distributed benefits are accounted for, using hydrogen for peak storage may be worthwhile, particularly in [areas] with transmission constraints (such as Los Angeles, San Francisco, Chicago, New York City, and Long Island). Such applications may be able to justify capital costs upwards of $4,000/kW [kilowatt]. Another attractive use of large-scale hydrogen storage would be in places like New Zealand or Brazil, whose hydroelectric systems have too little storage (12 weeks in NZ) to provide resilience against drought—but whose snowmelt or rainy seasons provide cheap surplus hydropower that could be stored as hydrogen, even in old gas-fields.

Many people assume that fuel makes more electricity if burned in an efficient power plant than if converted into hydrogen and then used in a fuel cell. This is not necessarily true. For example, using gasified biomass in a high-temperature molten-carbonate fuel cell, which needs no reformer, looks economically promising, even though reforming the biomass into hydrogen would be only about 60–65% efficient—worse than for reforming natural gas. . . .

## Myth

*We don't have practical ways to run cars on gaseous hydrogen, so cars must continue to use liquid fuels.*

Turning wheels with electric motors has well-known advantages of torque, ruggedness, reliability, simplicity, controllability, quietness, and low cost. Heavy and costly batteries have limited battery-powered electric cars to small niche markets, although the miniature lithium batteries now used in cellphones are severalfold better than the batteries used in electric

*Some experts believe that the majority of internal combustion engines, such as the one that drives the hybrid Ford Focus, will be powered by fuel cells in the near future.*

cars. But California regulators' initial focus on battery cars had a huge societal value because it greatly advanced electric drivesystems. The only question is where to get the electricity. Hybrid-electric cars now on the market from Honda and Toyota, and soon from virtually all automakers, make the electricity with onboard engine-generators, or recover it from braking. These "hybrid-electric" designs provide all the advantages of electric propulsion without the disadvantages of batteries. Still better will be fuel cells—the most efficient (~50–70% from hydrogen to direct-current electricity), clean, and reliable known way to make electricity from fuel. Nearly all significant automakers now have major fuel-cell car development programs.

Remember the high-school chemistry experiment of electrolysis—splitting water with an electric current and making hydrogen and oxygen bubble out of the test-tube? Fuel cells reverse this process by chemically recombining hydrogen and oxygen on a special membrane, at temperatures as low as 160–190°F (much higher in some types). This electrochemical reaction, with no combustion, produces electricity, pure hot water suitable for a coffee machine in the dashboard, byproduct heat suitable for heating or cooling the vehicle, and nothing else. Invented in 1839, used in space shuttles since 1965, and demonstrated in a passenger vehicle (GM's *Electrovan*) in 1966, fuel cells have been widely used for decades in aerospace and military applications, where they're prized for their ruggedness, simplicity, and reliability. Now they're rapidly emerging as power sources for portable electronics and home appliances (such as hand tools and vacuum cleaners), due to market by 2004–05. Fuel cells are already competitive for buildings when installed in the right place and used in the right way. So are certain industrial niche markets.

In the past decade, breakthroughs in materials and manufacturing engineering have reduced the need for precious-metal catalysts (especially when using pure hydrogen) by more than 20-fold, and have raised the power density and cut the cost of the most common type of fuel cell by 10-fold. Continuing advances in both the fuel-cell "stack" and the other components in the fuel-cell system now make it realistic to expect fuel cells to start competing with grid electricity in general use (*i.e.*, at about $500–800/kW if no distributed benefits are counted) within this decade, and even with internal-combustion engines by around 2010 in carefully integrated vehicle designs needing ~$100–300/kW.

In the next few years, more durable membranes and manufacturable designs are widely expected to permit rapidly expanding mass production of fuel cells for both vehicles and buildings. Once those innovation triggers have occurred, then as for most other manufactured goods, real cost should fall by ~20–30% for each doubling of cumulative production until limited by the cost of the basic materials. In very high volumes, the projected production cost of a low-temperature fuel-cell stack can ultimately reach on the order of $30–60/kW, not far from the ~$20/kW cost of generator-equipped internal-combustion engines, which have been refined for more than a century and are produced in enormous volumes. . . . If they become durable first, enough can be made for buildings—which use two-thirds of U.S. electricity—to make them cheap enough for vehicles, while if they first become cheap enough for vehicles, they can also be used in buildings and renovated or replaced as needed. Either way, each market accelerates the other by building production volume, cutting cost, and creating profitable linkages.

# Hydrogen Technology Is Inefficient

## Frank Kreith and Ron West

In the following selection professors Frank Kreith and Ron West outline the reasons why hydrogen technology is not efficient enough to supply America's energy needs. The authors describe each method by which hydrogen can be produced and reject each as inefficient, costly, wasteful, or polluting. In their opinion, hydrogen is not likely to serve as the fuel of the future. Frank Kreith and Ron West are professors emeriti of chemical engineering at the University of Colorado, Boulder. Kreith is also a fellow at the American Society of Mechanical Engineers and has served as a White House energy adviser.

The purpose of this study is to ascertain whether or not technologies that are currently available or close to commercialization can fulfill these expectations and justify proposing hydrogen as the future fuel for our nation's economy. . . .

Hydrogen is abundant on Earth, but only in chemically bound form. In order to use hydrogen as a fuel, it is necessary that it be available in unbound form. As a consequence of chemical reaction energies involved, a substantial energy input is needed to obtain unbound hydrogen. This energy input exceeds the energy released by the same hydrogen when used as a fuel. For example, to split water into hydrogen and oxygen according to the reaction $H_2O \rightarrow H_2 + \frac{1}{2}O_2$, 120 MJ/kg [megajoule per kilogram]-hydrogen are needed (all gases at $25\,°C$); while the reverse reaction of combining hydrogen and oxygen to give water (all gases

Frank Kreith and Ron West, "Fallacies of a Hydrogen Economy: A Critical Analysis of Hydrogen Production and Utilization," *Journal of Energy Resources Technology*, vol. 126, December 2004. Copyright © 2004 by ASME. All rights reserved. Reproduced by permission.

Natural gas rigs like this one in Colorado provide much of the energy used in the United States. Natural gas is cheaper to produce and easier to distribute than hydrogen.

at 25°C), ideally yields 120 MJ/kg-hydrogen. But, because no real process can be 100% efficient, more than 120 MJ/kg must be added to the first reaction, while less than 120 MJ/kg of useful energy can be recovered from the recombination. To evaluate the losses, it is, therefore, necessary to examine the energetics of hydrogen production processes quantitatively. . . .

## Hydrogen Produced from Fossil Fuels via Chemical Reactions

Chemical conversions of fossil fuels to hydrogen, from natural gas and petroleum fractions in particular, are well-established, commercial technologies. The use of coal as a raw material for hydrogen production has been studied extensively, but it is not widely practiced in the U.S.

## How Current U.S. Hydrogen and Gasoline Production and Distribution Systems Compare

| | Hydrogen system | Gasoline system |
|---|---|---|
| Production | 9 million tons per year | 150 million tons per year |
| Pipeline capacity | Less than 700 miles | Approximately 200,000 miles |
| Distribution stations | Less than 15 stations | More than 175,000 |
| Delivery trucks | Approximately 19 hydrogen trucks to deliver the equivalent of one gasoline truck | |

Source: Energy Information Administration, www.eia.doe.gov, 2002.

*Hydrogen to Heat via Combustion.* . . . For low-pressure uses, such as generating electricity and home heating, the efficiency of delivering hydrogen is only about 69%, whereas it is 88% for natural gas. With a typical combustion efficiency of 85%, the efficiency of utilization of hydrogen is about 59%, compared to 76% for natural gas. Thus the efficiency of combusting hydrogen is about 29% lower than that for supplying the natural gas for the same purpose. This is due to the fact that the energy efficiency of converting natural gas to hydrogen and then storing, transmitting, and distributing it is low. For heat generation, hydrogen could be combusted at an efficiency of 85%, yielding an overall cradle-to-grave efficiency of 57% compared to natural gas combustion at 75%. Thus, to use hydrogen in this way would require 32% more natural gas and produce 32% more carbon dioxide pollution than burning the natural gas directly.

To supply compressed hydrogen as a fuel in conventional spark-injection engines, at 62% efficiency, requires about 32% more natural gas than it does to supply the natural gas directly as engine fuel, at 82% efficiency. To supply liquid hydrogen, at 57% efficiency, would require 44% more natural gas, and produce that much more carbon dioxide, than it would to supply the natural gas to spark-injection engines. This is because, even though hydrogen and natural gas burn with essentially the same efficiency in the engine, the compression or liquefaction of hydrogen for storage on a vehicle requires substantially more energy. Results for fossil fuels other than natural gas as hydrogen sources are even less favorable to hydrogen, because petroleum and coal are more difficult to convert to hydrogen than is natural gas.

It can be concluded that to make hydrogen from fossil fuels and then to burn the hydrogen for generating heat or fueling internal combustion engines is less efficient than using the fossil fuel directly.

*Hydrogen to Electricity.* . . . If electricity generated with hydrogen made from natural gas is used in a fuel cell to produce electricity, the overall well-to-grid efficiency of 35% is less than the well-to-grid efficiency of 38%, obtained by burning the hydrogen to produce electricity in a gas-turbine combined cycle. Either way, generating power for the grid with hydrogen is less efficient than burning the natural gas directly, for which a well-to-grid power generation efficiency of 48% can be achieved with present technology. Results for other fossil fuels are similar. It can be seen, therefore, that the use of hydrogen generated from fossil fuels to produce electricity uses more fossil fuel and generates more carbon dioxide than generating electricity from fossil fuel directly. It may be concluded that the use of hydrogen made from fossil fuel to generate electricity for the grid is wasteful and increases carbon dioxide emissions. . . .

## Hydrogen Produced from Fossil, Nuclear, and Renewable Sources via Thermolysis

Thermolysis is splitting of water into hydrogen and oxygen by heating it. The heat can come from fossil, nuclear, or renewable sources. The production of hydrogen by thermolysis has been explored in detail. It was found that, because water is a very stable substance, only at temperatures higher than 3000°C (5400°F) does the equilibrium reaction significantly favor its decomposition into hydrogen and oxygen. Although a catalyst might increase the rate of reaction, it cannot change the reaction equilibrium. Hence, an extremely high temperature is required, because the equilibrium versus temperature relationship is fixed by the chemical reaction. In principle, the reaction can be driven at somewhat lower temperatures by separating the hydrogen and oxygen from the water as they are formed. But unless the hydrogen and oxygen are separated from each other at the reaction temperature, they will react back to water as the mixture is cooled. Separations at such high temperatures are not technically feasible because it is virtually impossible to find suitable materials to be employed in the necessary hardware.

Therefore, it can be concluded that thermolysis of water is technically not a practical way to produce hydrogen, no matter what source of heat is used. . . .

## Hydrogen Produced from Fossil, Nuclear, and Renewable Sources via Electrolysis

*Hydrogen to Heat via Combustion.* Hydrogen produced by electrolysis [the use of electric current to separate water in oxygen and hydrogen] could be used to produce heat by combustion. However, the efficiency of producing hydrogen from electricity by means of electrolysis is only about 70%, and burning the hydrogen at an efficiency of 85% yields heat with an overall efficiency of about 60%, while electricity can be converted to heat at essentially 100% efficiency. Thus it is concluded that to use hydrogen made by electrolysis to produce heat is inefficient and wasteful.

*Hydrogen to Electricity via Fuel Cell.* The use of electricity to generate hydrogen, and the use of this hydrogen to then generate electricity again via a fuel cell is . . . very inefficient because a sequence of steps is involved. . . . It would take 2.9kW h [kiloWatt hours] of electricity input to produce 1 kW h of electricity output with present technologies, while even with optimistic advanced efficiencies, 1.9 kW h of input are required to yield 1 kW h of output. The difference between input and

*A sign near an industrial hydrogen refueling station in Germany warns that the gas is explosive. Carrying the flammable gas onboard vehicles is a persistent safety concern.*

output electricity would be wasted. Thus, the output electricity would cost from 1.9 to 2.9 times the cost of the input electricity. Moreover, this cost ratio considers only the cost of the input electricity, and does not include the capital cost and non-electrical operating costs of the electrolysis, fuel cell, and hydrogen storage equipment. Also, it does not include the cost or energy necessary for compression or liquefaction of hydrogen for storage. Since these results do not depend on the source of the original electricity or upon the use of the electricity, the results also apply to using electricity to power a fuel-cell vehicle.

There may be niche applications where weight is a more important factor than cost, such as for space vehicles, or where incremental electricity available from stored hydrogen may be so valuable, such as at times of peak electricity demand, that the extra cost could be acceptable. However, such niche applications do not suggest a major role for hydrogen in a national energy policy.

This analysis shows that any path, no matter what the source of the original electricity, which uses electricity to produce hydrogen and a fuel cell to use this hydrogen to again generate electricity, has low energy efficiency and adverse economic impact. This means that a large portion of the original resource is being wasted, both in an energetic and an economic sense. Furthermore, because of the insufficiency of the process, pollution will increase.

It is concluded that any pathway that includes the conversion of electricity to hydrogen by electrolysis, and then conversion of the hydrogen to electricity via a fuel cell is inefficient and not a desirable basis for an economically and environmentally sound energy policy.

*Hydrogen to Electricity via Combined Cycle Power Plant.* The efficiency of converting hydrogen to electricity via a gas turbine combined-cycle [a turbine that combusts gas for power and uses the waste heat to generate steam for additional power] is about 55%. Though this is more efficient than present fuel cell systems, it is lower than the optimistic value for fuel cells. It is not expected that the combined-cycle efficiency will increase to the level of the optimistic fuel cell value. Since it has already been demonstrated that even the optimistic fuel cells are an inefficient way of using hydrogen produced by electrolysis, the use of hydrogen in a combined cycle power plant, that is even less efficient, is clearly not desirable. Therefore, it is concluded that the conversion of electricity to hydrogen and using hydrogen to generate electricity via a combined cycle power plant is inefficient and is not a desirable process for an energy policy.

# Hydrogen-Powered Cars Are Viable

## Tom Nicholls

Tom Nicholls is the editor of *Petroleum Economist*, an international energy journal. In the following article Nicholls reports that the commercial use of hydrogen fuel—especially in cars—is imminent. As Nicholls explains, fuel cell technology is advancing, and automobile makers have already committed large sums of money to develop hydrogen-powered vehicles. In addition, Nicholls writes that the U.S. government's support for the conversion to hydrogen energy is speeding the automakers' plans. Nicholls acknowledges that hydrogen fuel cell technology is still in its infancy, but he notes that several automakers have announced that they expect hydrogen cars to became viable alternatives to gasoline vehicles sometime between 2010 and 2020.

Progress in commercialising hydrogen technology is advancing rapidly. Stationary fuel cells could be supplying domestic energy needs as early as next year [2004], while hydrogen-powered cars could be on sale by the end of the decade.

Fuel cells, in which hydrogen and oxygen combine in an electrochemical reaction to produce water, generating electricity, are surprisingly close to commercial application. Cars powered by hydrogen could be available as soon as 2010 and in widespread use by 2020. Stationary fuel cells, for supplying energy to businesses and homes, are much closer to becoming a profitable business proposition—manufacturers hope to start selling products around the middle of the decade.

Momentum in the research and development (R&D) process—dominated by Japan, Europe and North America—suggests the economics of fuel cells are promising. Energy companies are forming business units dedicated to hydrogen and putting financial muscle into R&D. Rivalry among the world's main car companies to produce the first affordable and reliable fuel cell car is intense. Governments are supplying more and more funding.

## Government Support

The US government gave fuel cells . . . a significant boost in January [2003], when hydrogen technology formed an important part of President George [W.] Bush's State of the Union speech. Bush said the government would provide $1.7bn [billion]

*In his 2003 State of the Union address, President George W. Bush pledged more than a billion dollars to fund fuel cell research and development over a five year period.*

(including $0.72bn in new spending) for R&D funding for vehicles and stationary units over the next five years.

The rewards for all could be considerable in terms of efficiency, the environment and energy supply security.

According to UTC Fuel Cells (UTCFC), one of the world's main fuel cell manufacturers, electrical efficiency is 40%, rising to 80% if the heat is also recovered. Fuel efficiency in fuel cell cars is also much higher than in conventional vehicles. In terms of operation (tank-to-wheel efficiency), a fuel cell is about twice as efficient as a gasoline-fired internal combustion engine. In addition, it is generally thought that overall efficiency, taking into account the source of the hydrogen (well-to-wheel efficiency), can also be higher. . . .

## Public-Private Partnership

The extra US government spending—allocated under the FreedomCAR (Cooperative Automotive Research) and Fuel Initiative (FFI)—builds on FreedomCAR, a partnership between the government and the private sector founded in early 2002 with the aim of making fuel cell cars commonplace in the US by 2020 and cost-competitive with gasoline vehicles by 2010. The DOE [Department of Energy] estimates FFI could reduce GHG [greenhouse gas] emissions from transportation in the US by over 0.5bn tonnes of carbon equivalent a year by 2040, with additional reductions resulting from the use of fuel cells in other applications. It could also represent important energy supply security for the US by reducing its dependence—a national priority—on foreign sources of oil. The DOE believes oil imports could be cut by over 11m [million] b/d [barrels per day] by 2040 (at present, imports amount to 10m–11m b/d).

> ### ANOTHER OPINION
>
> ### The Case for Hydrogen Cars
>
> The case for hydrogen is threefold. First, hydrogen fuel cell vehicles appear to be a superior consumer product desired by the automotive industry. Second . . ., the potential exists for dramatic reductions in the cost of hydrogen production, distribution, and use. And third, hydrogen provides the potential for zero tailpipe pollution, near-zero well-to-wheels emissions of greenhouse gases, and the elimination of oil imports, simultaneously addressing the most vexing challenges facing the fuels sector, well beyond what could be achieved with hybrid vehicles and energy efficiency.
>
> Daniel Sperling and Joan Ogden, *Issues in Science & Technology*, Spring 2004.

In order to attain the various desirable end-results, there is a lot of work still to do. For a start, hydrogen, when produced from natural gas, is four times as expensive to produce as gasoline, according to the DOE.

## Making Fuel Cells Affordable

Government subsidies will reinforce the technology's economics, but affordability remains the biggest stumbling block, along

*Pictured is a Honda FCX. Honda and Toyota were the first automakers to offer fuel cell vehicles in U.S. markets.*

with durability and reliability. Stationary units are the closest to market entry. There are several types of fuel cell with a variety of possible applications, but attention is focused on the Proton Exchange Membrane (PEM) system (also called Polymer Electrolyte Fuel Cell system—PEFC). Compared with other types of fuel cell, PEM units are smaller, easier to manufacture, operate at much lower temperatures and have greater commercial possibilities, such as supplying homes. They are being developed for cars, so scientific breakthroughs in the automotive field can be transferred to stationary applications, streamlining research and reducing costs. In the production phase, cost savings through mass production in the auto industry can also be transferred to the stationary sector.

## Reliable and Affordable

"We will be able to make a practical, reliable and affordable fuel cell by 2005," says Toshiya Ohmura, manager of the Japan Gas Association's (JGA) fuel cell and hydrogen project department. JGA is taking an active role in R&D and aims to promote the use of fuel cells powered by hydrogen produced from natural gas. . . .

The problems for fuel cell car manufacturers are even greater [than affordability]. Part of the difficulty of successfully marketing fuel cell cars is that conventional gasoline and diesel cars have become so sophisticated in performance and cost. They will inevitably be the benchmark for hydrogen cars and, if they do not match up, consumers will not buy them.

In technical terms, operating conditions are much more onerous and space is restricted. "The environment under which a fuel cell must perform in a car is much more harrowing than a stationary application, which does not move and starts and stops once every few months," says [Jim] Bolch [vice president of UTCFC]. "In a car, it needs to be able to provide acceleration, deal with cold weather, hot weather, vibration and people driving their cars up onto the pavement. It is a much more challenging environment."

## Commercial Viability by 2010

Although significant savings will come from mass production, cost-reductions are essential—Honda says the cost of producing a fuel cell car is 100 times the cost of producing a conventional vehicle. "We expect fuel cell cars to be commercial in 10–20 years from now," a company spokesman says, but adds that there "must be a technical breakthrough" before they can enter widespread use. Similarly, DaimlerChrysler expects "a broad market entry" of fuel cell vehicles after 2010.

The Japanese government also expects rapid expansion in the fuel cell car marketplace in the next decade. Its target for fuel cell cars in the domestic market is 50,000 by 2010 out of a total population of 70m cars and for 5m vehicles by 2020.

Car companies are taking a range of different approaches to fuel cells. In Honda's vehicles, a fuel cell powers the car using hydrogen stored in a tank. Toyota is developing hybrid vehicles that have an electric motor powered by a fuel cell and by a secondary battery, a system it claims has a superior well-to-wheel efficiency to that of vehicles powered only by fuel cells. Germany's BMW, meanwhile, has adopted a very different approach and is trying to develop an internal-combustion engine that burns hydrogen instead of fossil fuels. A separate fuel cell in the same vehicle would power the car's electrical devices. Given the lack of hydrogen refuelling facilities, the firm is developing so-called dual-fuel cars. These are able to run off gasoline or hydrogen and are fitted with separate tanks for each fuel.

## The Need for Refuelling Networks

Regardless of the system individual companies adopt, hydrogen vehicles also need refuelling networks, which will be expensive to build. Alternatives are: refuelling stations that use methane (or other hydrocarbons) as a feedstock, which is reformed on site, allowing vehicles to be filled directly with hydrogen; [steam] reforming systems sited on board vehicles that fill up with hydrocarbons; or, if fuel cells are widely distributed among households, cars could be charged at home. Initially, cars will refuel with hydrogen. This will require improvements in compression technology so that cars can drive a reasonable distance without having to refuel (as a light gas, hydrogen's energy density is much lower than that of liquid fuels).

On-board reforming is an attractive option for the longer term as it limits the need for new hydrogen infrastructure and on-board hydrogen compression, but it would be technically very difficult because of the operating conditions. "With on-board reforming, you are asking a vehicle to behave like a refinery and it is a challenging chemical-engineering issue to get everything to work in a small space, the way you want it to work. Reforming itself is not difficult, but doing it in real-time and enabling the car to respond to the needs of a driver are considerable challenges," says David Jollie, editor, *Fuel Cell Today*.

According to Jollie, all the refuelling systems are possible and will depend on market circumstances, which may vary from region to region. "The various systems all have separate benefits and it is not impossible for all of them to be used. It will be a question of what the market pull is and what the interests of energy companies, customers and car companies are."

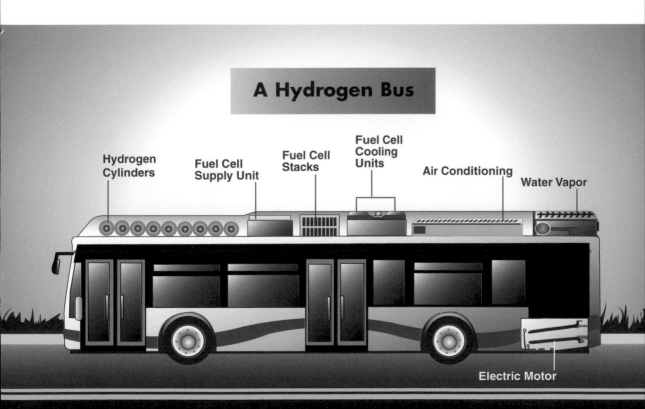

**A Hydrogen Bus**

Hydrogen Cylinders — Fuel Cell Supply Unit — Fuel Cell Stacks — Fuel Cell Cooling Units — Air Conditioning — Water Vapor — Electric Motor

Source: Transport for London, www.tfl.gov.uk.

The infrastructure problem gives buses an advantage over cars, because they usually need only one, centralised fuelling point. As a result, they are likely to be commercialised first. UTCFC, for example, expects fleet vehicles to become an emerging market "in the 2005–2007 time-frame".

Fuel-cell bus programmes are driving the hydrogen R&D effort in Europe. The European Union's (EU) Euro 18.5m ($19.9m) Clean Urban Transport for Europe demonstration project aims to help nine European cities introduce hydrogen into their public transportation system. The EU says the project, the largest fuel-cell bus demonstration project in the world, will address the issues of hydrogen production, refuelling in city centres and operational use in commercial public-transport systems. Buses will operate like normal buses, on the same lines and under the same tight time schedule to provide the best comparisons of performance and cost.

As part of Iceland's plan to become the world's first hydrogen economy, the Ectos project, which is being run by Icelandic New Energy (a business partnership involving DaimlerChrysler, Norsk Hydro and Royal Dutch/Shell), is introducing three fuel cell buses to the public transport network. If tests are successful, Ectos' aim is to replace "a larger number" of Reykjavik city buses with hydrogen vehicles. . . .

Many other fuel cell popularisation programmes exist. Among the most important in North America is California Fuel Cell Partnership (CaFCP). The venture involves car, energy and fuel cell companies, and government agencies. CaFCP aims to have up to 60 fuel cell vehicles on the road by the end of 2003 (which will include some buses).[1] Its main aims are to: demonstrate the vehicle technology by operating and testing under real-world conditions in California; demonstrate the viability of alternative fuel infrastructure technology, including hydrogen and methanol stations; explore the path to commercialisation, from identifying potential problems to developing solutions; and increase public awareness and enhance opinion about fuel cell electric vehicles, preparing the market for commercialisation.

1. The CaFCP has tested fifty-five cars in California and in 2005 experimented with a few buses on select routes.

# Hydrogen-Powered Cars Will Not Appear Soon

## Joseph Romm

Joseph Romm is a former deputy assistant secretary of energy (1995–1998). Romm gave the following testimony to the House of Representatives Science Committee during its review of the FreedomCAR Initiative, a national agenda to research clean fuels. Romm contends that the nation should not pursue hydrogen-powered vehicles because hydrogen fuel cell engines are inefficient and expensive when compared to gasoline or hybrid engines. In addition, the energy sources used to charge hydrogen fuel cells are mainly fossil fuels that contribute to pollution and global warming. According to Romm, the country should focus on combating global warming in the short term, a goal that cannot, in his view, be achieved by investing in fossil-fuel-derived hydrogen energy.

Hydrogen and fuel cell cars are being hyped today as few technologies have ever been. . . .

Yet, for all the hype, a number of recent studies raise serious doubts about the prospects for hydrogen cars. In February 2004, a prestigious National Academy of Sciences panel concluded, "In the best-case scenario, the transition to a hydrogen economy would take many decades, and any reductions in oil imports and carbon dioxide emissions are likely to be minor during the next 25 years." And that's the best case. Realistically, . . . a major effort to introduce hydrogen cars before 2030 would undermine

Joseph Romm, testimony submitted to the U.S. House of Representatives, House Science Committee, March 3, 2004.

efforts to reduce emissions of heat-trapping greenhouse gases like carbon dioxide—the main culprit in last century's planet-wide warming of 1 degree Fahrenheit.

As someone who helped oversee the Department of Energy's [DOE] program for clean energy, including hydrogen, for much of the 1990s—during which time we increased hydrogen funding by a factor of ten . . . —I believe that continued research into hydrogen remains important because of its potential to provide a pollution-free substitute for oil in the second half of this century. But if we fail to limit greenhouse gas emissions over the next decade—and especially if we fail to do so because we have bought into the hype about hydrogen's near-term prospects—we will be making an unforgivable national blunder that may lock in global warming for the U.S. of 1 degree Fahrenheit *per decade* by mid-century. . . .

## Fuel Cells

The most promising [hydrogen] fuel cell for transportation is the Proton Exchange Membrane (PEM) fuel cell. . . . The price goal for transportation fuel cells is to come close to that of an internal combustion engine, roughly $30 per kilowatt. Current PEM costs are about 100 times greater. It has taken wind power and solar power each about twenty years to see a tenfold decline in prices, after major government and private-sector investments in R&D, and they still each comprise well under 1% of U.S. electricity generation. A major technology breakthrough is needed in transportation fuel cells before they will be practical.

Running a fuel cell car on pure hydrogen, the option now being pursued by most automakers and fuel cell companies, means the car must be able to safely, compactly, and cost-effectively store hydrogen onboard. This is a major technical challenge. At room temperature and pressure, hydrogen takes up some 3,000 times more space than gasoline containing an equivalent amount of energy. The Department of Energy's 2003 *Fuel Cell Report to Congress* notes:

> Hydrogen storage systems need to enable a vehicle to travel 300 to 400 miles and fit in an envelope that does not compromise either passenger space or storage space. Current energy storage technologies are insufficient to gain market acceptance because they do not meet these criteria.

The most mature storage options are liquefied hydrogen and compressed hydrogen gas.

Liquid hydrogen is widely used today for storing and transporting hydrogen. . . .

Liquid hydrogen [however] is exceedingly unlikely to be a major part of a hydrogen economy because of the cost and logistical problems in handling liquid hydrogen and because liquefaction is so energy intensive. Some 40% of the energy of the hydrogen is required to liquefy it for storage. Liquefying one kg of hydrogen using electricity from the U.S. grid would by itself release some 18 to 21 pounds of carbon dioxide into the atmosphere, roughly equal to the carbon dioxide emitted by burning one gallon of gasoline.

Compressed hydrogen storage is used by nearly all prototype hydrogen vehicles today. Hydrogen is compressed up to pressures of 5,000 pounds per square inch (psi) or even 10,000 psi in a multistage process that requires energy input equal to 10% to 15% of the hydrogen's usable energy content. For comparison, atmospheric pressure is about 15 psi.

Working at such high pressures creates overall system complexity and requires materials and components that are sophisticated and costly. And even a 10,000-psi tank would take up 7 to 8 times the volume of an equivalent-energy gasoline tank or perhaps four times the volume for a comparable range (since the fuel cell vehicle will be more fuel efficient than current cars).

The National Academy study concluded that both liquid and compressed storage have "little promise of long-term practicality for light-duty

Andy Singer. Reproduced by permission.

# Hydrogen Cars Pollute More than Conventional Vehicles

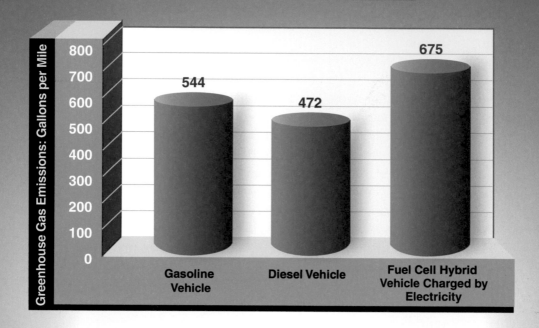

Greenhouse Gas Emissions: Gallons per Mile

- Gasoline Vehicle: 544
- Diesel Vehicle: 472
- Fuel Cell Hybrid Vehicle Charged by Electricity: 675

# Hydrogen Cars Use More Energy than Conventional Vehicles

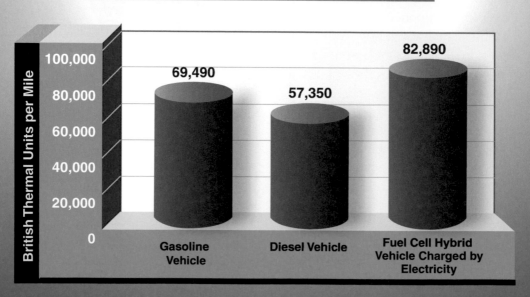

British Thermal Units per Mile

- Gasoline Vehicle: 69,490
- Diesel Vehicle: 57,350
- Fuel Cell Hybrid Vehicle Charged by Electricity: 82,890

Source: General Motors, Argonne National Laboratory, BO, ExxonMobil, and Shell, "Well-to-Wheel Energy Use and Greenhouse Gas Emissions of Advanced Fuel/Vehicle Systems—North American Analysis," www.energyindependencenow.org, June 2001.

vehicles" and recommended that DOE halt research in both areas. Practical hydrogen storage requires a major technology breakthrough, most likely in solid-state hydrogen storage.

## An Unusually Dangerous Fuel

Hydrogen has some safety advantages over liquid fuels like gasoline. When a gasoline tank leaks or bursts, the gasoline can pool, creating a risk that any spark would start a fire, or it can splatter, posing a great risk of spreading an existing fire. Hydrogen, however, will escape quickly into the atmosphere as a very diffuse gas. Also, hydrogen gas is non-toxic.

Yet, hydrogen has its own major safety issues. It is highly flammable with an ignition energy 20 times smaller than that of natural gas or gasoline. It can be ignited by cell phones and electrical storms located miles away. Hence, leaks pose a significant fire hazard. . . .

## The High Cost of Fuel and Infrastructure

A key problem with the hydrogen economy is that pollution-free sources of hydrogen are unlikely to be practical and affordable for decades. Indeed, even the pollution-generating means of making hydrogen are currently too expensive and too inefficient to substitute for oil. . . .

Another key issue is the chicken-and-egg problem: Who will spend the hundreds of billions of dollars on a wholly new nationwide infrastructure to provide ready access to hydrogen for consumers with fuel-cell vehicles until millions of hydrogen vehicles are on the road? Yet who will manufacture and market such vehicles until the infrastructure is in place to fuel those vehicles? And will car companies and fuel providers be willing to take this chance before knowing whether the public will embrace these cars? . . .

Centralized production of hydrogen is the ultimate goal. A pure hydrogen economy requires that hydrogen be generated from carbon-dioxide-free sources, which would almost certainly require centralized hydrogen production closer to giant wind-farms or at coal/biomass gasification power plants where carbon dioxide is extracted for permanent underground storage. That will require some way of delivering massive quantities of hydrogen to tens of thousands of local fueling stations. . . .

Producing hydrogen on-site at local fueling stations is the strategy advocated by those who want to deploy hydrogen vehicles in the next two decades. On-site electrolysis is impractical for large-scale use because it would be highly expensive and inefficient, while generating large amounts of greenhouse gases and other pollutants. The hydrogen would need to be generated from small methane reformers. Although onsite methane reforming seems viable for limited demonstrations and pilots, it is also both impractical and unwise for large-scale application, for a number of reasons.

First, the upfront cost is very high—more than $600 billion just to provide hydrogen fuel for 40% of the cars on the road, according to Argonne [National Labs]. A reasonable cost estimate for the initial hydrogen infrastructure, derived from Royal Dutch/Shell figures, is $5000 per car.

Second, the cost of the delivered hydrogen itself in this option is also higher than for centralized production. Not only are the small reformers and compressors typically more expensive and less efficient than larger units, but they will likely pay a much higher price for the electricity and gas to run them. A 2002 analysis put the cost at $4.40 per kg (that is, equal to $4.40 per gallon of gasoline). . . .

## Global Warming Issues

Perhaps the ultimate reason hydrogen cars are a post-2030 technology is the growing threat of global warming. Our energy choices are now inextricably tied to the fate of our global climate. The burning of fossil fuels—oil, gas and coal—emits carbon dioxide ($CO_2$) into the atmosphere where it builds up, blankets the earth and traps heat, accelerating global warming. We now have greater concentrations of

$CO_2$ in the atmosphere than at any time in the past 420,000 years, and probably anytime in the past 3 million years—leading to rising global temperatures, more extreme weather events (including floods and droughts), sea level rise, the spread of tropical diseases, and the destruction of crucial habitats, such as coral reefs.

Unfortunately, the path set by the current energy policy of the U.S. and developing world will dramatically *increase* emissions over the next few decades, which will force sharper and more painful reductions in the future when we finally do act. Global $CO_2$ emissions are projected to rise more than 50% by 2030. From 2001 to 2025, the U.S. Energy Information Administration (EIA) projects a 40% increase in U.S. coal consumption for electricity generation. And the U.S. transportation sector is projected to generate nearly half of the 40% rise in U.S. $CO_2$ emissions forecast for 2025, which again is long before hydrogen-powered cars could have a positive impact on greenhouse gas emissions.

Two points are clear. First, we cannot wait for hydrogen cars to address global warming. Second, we should not pursue a strategy to reduce greenhouse gas emissions in the transportation sector that would undermine efforts to reduce greenhouse gas emissions in the electric generation sector. Yet that is precisely what a hydrogen-car strategy would do for the next few decades.

For near-term deployment, hydrogen would almost certainly be produced from fossil fuels. Yet running a fuel-cell car on such hydrogen in 2020 would offer no significant life-cycle greenhouse gas advantage over the 2004 [Toyota] Prius [hybrid automobile] running on gasoline. . . .

We shouldn't be rushing to deploy hydrogen cars in the next two decades anyway, since not only are several R&D breakthroughs required, we also need a revolution in clean energy that dramatically accelerates the penetration rates of new $CO_2$-neutral electricity. Hydrogen cars might find limited value replacing diesel engines (for example, in buses) in very polluted cities before 2030, but they are unlikely to achieve mass-market commercialization by then. That is why I conclude neither government policy nor business investment should be based on the belief that hydrogen cars will have meaningful commercial success in the near- or medium-term.

# CHAPTER 3

# How Feasible Is a Future Hydrogen Economy?

# America Should Convert to a Hydrogen Economy

**Terry Backer**

Terry Backer is a representative in the Connecticut legislature. He chairs the Connecticut House Energy and Technology Committee and is also the vice chair of the National Conference of State Legislatures' Energy Committee. In the following article he explains why his state and the nation should adopt a grand-scale hydrogen fuel program. Backer claims that a hydrogen economy would free Americans from dependence on foreign oil. Although he acknowledges that hydrogen fuel technology is still expensive and unproven, Backer asserts that building hydrogen fueling stations and continuing to develop better fuel cells will ensure that the United States will not remain at the mercy of foreign oil markets.

Five-dollar-a-gallon gasoline.

It's no stretch of the imagination anymore. In fact, it's just shy of becoming a reality. In some countries it's already here. And if that number gives you a chill then that same price for heating oil may very well cause you to freeze. The American economy and the consumer have had their chest laid bare to the world market's competition for energy locked in natural gas and oil.

Yet, it doesn't have to be that way. Science, technology and world political events have brought us to the place we need to be. This confluence of factors brings us to the eve of a much

Terry Backer, "Freedom from Fossil Fuels," *State Legislatures*, vol. 31, February 2005. Reproduced by permission.

needed revolution in America, an energy revolution. However, in order for the public good to prevail over deeply rooted multinational interest, the people must once again join forces to lead it.

## Failure to Lead

In many ways our government has failed our country. It has not in any meaningful way helped develop and create the alternative energy infrastructure we need to pull away from oil and all its attendant political and environmental ills. Instead lawmakers have relied on the world's energy producers to set policy and provide information on the very matter that enriches them. Government has given short shrift to a vast array of new technologies that can provide the energy we rely on for our society. In some ways it has even stifled the creation of incentives needed to move the process along.

Energy, most of it produced from oil distillates, is a huge cost driver for each of us on an individual level as well as for business and industry. It's not that the world will run out of oil any time soon. It's not clear if oil production has peaked although some noted experts think it may have.

But the demand for energy is growing worldwide at a rate not anticipated 20 years ago. Supplies of deeper more difficult to reach reservoirs of oil are more costly to extract. If we learned anything from our high school economics class it is the rule of supply and demand. A greater demand coupled with a lower supply results in higher costs. Supply is contracting worldwide (or the cost of obtaining that supply is increasing). Demand is growing at unprecedented rates in Asia and elsewhere. That equals higher prices for all of us at the pump and the light switch. Not to mention all our goods and services. China is an example of the world's changing economy, although China is certainly not the only rapidly developing country voraciously consuming the world's oil reserves.

## A Look at China

The economic growth in China is the fastest in the world. China's Gross Domestic Product [GDP] grew by the rate of 9.1

percent in 2002, and to the increasingly alarming 9.7 percent within the first half of 2004. To put this into perspective, the U.S. GDP has averaged about 3.3 percent over the last 12 years.

China is the second largest importer of oil, second only to the United States. The United States now imports 64 percent of its oil and remains the largest consumer of oil products. We are 4 percent of the world's population. The other 5.6 billion or so people want the things we have: refrigerators and automobiles, things that need energy. Over the past 75 or so years, the United States and Western Europe were the primary developing nations. As such, most of the world's oil supply was ours to command since no one else had very many cars and trucks. This is rapidly changing. In June 2004, China imported 2.8 million

*Those who support a hydrogen economy argue that high gas prices represent just one of the many problems Americans will face as a result of continued dependence on oil.*

barrels of oil per day, a 47 percent increase over the preceding June of 2003 with no end in sight.

There is no silver bullet in the technological arsenal that will instantly offset oil as a primary transportation fuel or for energy needs across the board. In all likelihood, different types of alternatives will be used for various applications. That's good. A diversity of fuels for various applications can help reduce dependency and vulnerability to adverse economic and political situations. Geothermal, solar and wind will play important roles in shaving oil imports, but the automobile doesn't work very well on these technologies. It is the automobile that we must address if we are to find energy independency for our nation.

## Hope in Hydrogen

Hydrogen fuel cell powered vehicles are where the future lies. Hydrogen is the most plentiful element on the planet. It is found in every glass of water, in natural gas and even in landfill gas-sewage. This is not new technology. Sir William Robert Grove invented the fuel cell in the 1830s. Grove knew that by using electricity he could split water into hydrogen and oxygen. He theorized if you reversed the process and combined hydrogen and oxygen you would get electricity. He tried it. It worked. It still works today and after billions of dollars in investment and research, fuel cell buses and vehicles are on the road. Even more advanced models of fuel cell powered vehicles using the hybrid energy recovery systems like that used on the Honda Insight hybrid

*The Hangman's Noose.*

Paul Conrad. Reproduced by permission.

are being developed by automakers and companies like Connecticut's own United Technologies Company.

Sir William wasn't concerned about any number of other pluses that hydrogen fuel cells also bring to the table. They are more efficient users of fuel because nothing is being burned. The waste products from the process are water and heat, two byproducts that can be used again. Fuel cells are almost nonpolluting, the supply is abundant on earth and when made from water, as opposed to natural gas, the energy source is renewable.

It does take energy to make hydrogen. There is no free lunch. It takes about the same amount of energy used to refine oil into gasoline and heating fuels. When using natural gas, which has lots of hydrogen in it, fuel cells work just fine. The fuel cells can't really be called renewable sources of energy when used with natural gas, but it is a bridge fuel to hydrogen generation. The cells, when used with natural gas, are far more efficient in fuel-to-energy conversion than gasoline or other combustion engines and they can be called Green, very Green [not damaging to the environment].

Automobile manufacturers have developed fuel cell/hydrogen vehicles, and a few are already in use. But the technology can't be expanded until we start producing hydrogen fuel.

We face a chicken and egg situation when it comes to implementing fuel cell technology for our cars and trucks. The auto industry says there are no fueling stations to make the huge investment in setting up mass production and no one will build them because there is no mass manufacturing of fuel cell cars. Remember vinyl records? When the compact disc hit the market it was expected to take 15 years to penetrate because no one had CD players. Well, they just made the players and the CDs at the same time and records went the way of the Edsel [an obsolete automobile].

## Hydrogen Highways

Governor Arnold Schwarzenegger is breaking some eggs in California. He has proposed the world's first hydrogen highways.

He is involving business, nonprofit groups and technical experts in developing the blueprint. A map of the routes and technical requirements was due the first of the year [2005]. The plan calls for a public/private partnership to create and fund the system. Funding is expected to include a combination of revenue bonds, general fund appropriations and private money.

Fueling stations will be built along California's vast highway system as a public investment. Schwarzenegger is taking the first giant leap to make our energy revolution happen. In many ways, he is leading the nation's energy policy by taking action that protects us from being dependent on outside sources of energy. It seems if Washington can't or won't, Governor Schwarzenegger will. We [in Connecticut] can as well.

Fuel cells and some other alternatives are currently more expensive than the old oil driven machines, hence the reluctance to build the foundation. In a short time the world compe-

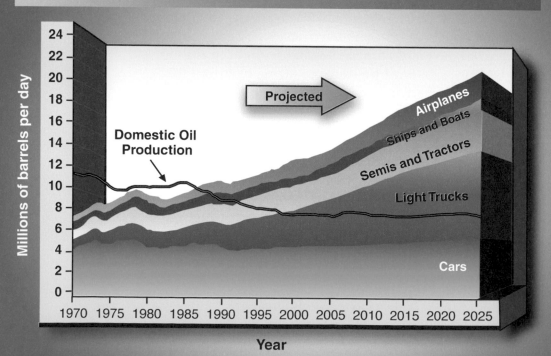

Source: Center for Transportation Analysis, *Transportation Energy Data Book: Edition 22*, September 2002, and Energy Information Administration, *EIA Annual Energy Outlook 2003*, January 2003.

*In 2004 California governor Arnold Schwarzenegger inaugurates the California Hydrogen Highways Network. The governor and General Motors vice chairman Bob Lutz (inset) fill up at one of the network's filling stations.*

tition for oil will drive prices even higher and fuel cells will become competitive and in short order cheaper than oil. We need to build the infrastructure now so industry can do its magic. We need to do as California is doing. Our energy flank is wide open to world market oil cost that can damage our economy and each of our pocketbooks.

Energy independence is freedom from foreign countries, their entanglements and multinational oil companies that don't really care about our country. In fact, the energy revolution may be the most patriotic thing we can do for our nation. As the founders of this country did 200 plus years ago we must now do as well—separate ourselves from foreign lords. Energy independence can be achieved. It will require public investment and putting the people's future first. We just need to be willing to invest in a future that is right around the corner.

# America Should Not Forgo Other Energy Alternatives to Pursue Hydrogen

## Bill Eggertson

Bill Eggertson is the executive director of the Canadian Association for Renewable Energies and the content director of *Refocus*, an international renewable energy magazine. In the following article from that periodical, Eggertson complains that the current push to develop hydrogen power is overshadowing investment in other renewable energy sources. According to Eggertson, the hydrogen economy is still a long way off, so developing hydrogen technologies should not be so heavily emphasized. Other renewable energy sources such as wind and solar power are presently feasible energy alternatives, and the United States should invest more heavily in them, he contends.

A number of fuel sources have been predicting their renaissance from the much-touted global transition to a hydrogen economy, but the transition will take many decades under the best-case scenario, concludes an analysis from the U.S. National Research Council [NRC]. Despite the US$1.2 billion funding announced [in 2003] by President George [W.] Bush, as well as significant funding by the European Community and other countries, the initiative to develop hydrogen as the fuel of the future has "technological and economic challenges to overcome," as well as a need to address concerns about costs, environmental impacts and safety.

"Our study suggests that, while hydrogen is a potential long-term energy approach for the nation, the government should keep a balanced portfolio of research and development efforts to enhance U.S. energy efficiency and develop alternative energy sources," explains Michael Ramage, who chaired the NRC "Committee on Alternatives & Strategies for Future Hydrogen Production & Use."

It bears repeating that hydrogen is a carrier . . . not an energy source, in the same way that electricity is not a fuel. Hydrogen is referred to as the most abundant element on earth, implying that

*Natural gas plants are a mainstay of America's energy supply. Some critics warn that using natural gas to make hydrogen will overburden these vital gas resources.*

it is as inexhaustible as cold fusion was trumpeted almost 15 years ago. However, most of the current supply of hydrogen is derived from natural gas, which increasingly is the 'fuel of choice' for the generation of electricity and thermal heating applications. Hydrogen can also be produced from nuclear and coal, as well as from renewables, but its widespread use will require cost-effective production "either in large plants or in smaller facilities," the report notes. The former would need significant infrastructure for distribution, while the latter would provide a good match for the distributed generation capabilities of renewables. . . .

## Ignoring Warnings About Hydrogen Energy

For the past two years, the renewable energy industry has anguished over the apparent strategy to transform much of the world's energy consumption into a hydrogen format that can be

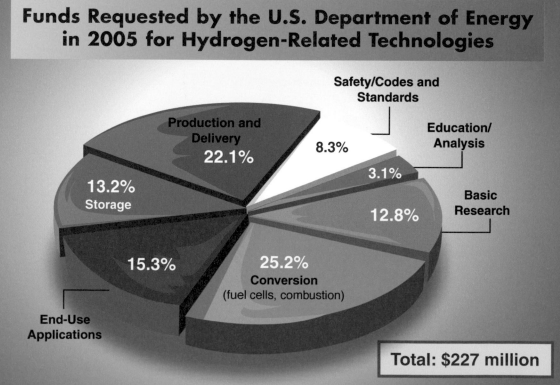

**Funds Requested by the U.S. Department of Energy in 2005 for Hydrogen-Related Technologies**

- Production and Delivery 22.1%
- Safety/Codes and Standards 8.3%
- Education/Analysis 3.1%
- Basic Research 12.8%
- Storage 13.2%
- End-Use Applications 15.3%
- Conversion (fuel cells, combustion) 25.2%

Total: $227 million

Source: U.S. Department of Energy, *Hydrogen Posture Plan*, www.eere.energy.gov, 2004.

used in fuel cells. That vision would allow this 'new energy' to meet most applications of green power, green fuel and green heat, but it ignores a number of factors. For instance, it is not obvious if the promoters of this evolution have insider knowledge about the future availability of natural gas (assuming it remains the predominant feedstock for hydrogen), but the report reminds U.S. politicians that 10% of that country's gas is imported now, and that level will increase significantly in future. "While the most cost-effective source of hydrogen for the long run is probably natural gas, its long-term use as a source of hydrogen would not increase U.S. energy independence," it warns.

Nor would large-scale conversion to hydrogen reduce climate-linked emissions to the level that most people have been led to believe, based on the marketing hype that hydrogen is a 'clean' energy. Many regions of the world, including the United States, have significant reserves of coal, and there is intensive lobbying to use this fossil fuel as the mainstay of hydrogen, tied in with carbon sequestration techniques to reduce GHG [greenhouse gas] emissions. Of course, hydrogen would be almost emission-free if it were produced from nuclear reactors or hydroelectric dams, and those technologies have also been preparing to boost their market share, based on the headlong rush to evolve the conversion strategy.

> **ANOTHER OPINION**
>
> ### America Should Pursue a Range of Energy Sources
> The challenge is to intervene in the multitude of energy systems blanketing the Earth to capture energy for the service of humankind. Wind turbines spread across the hills of California are producing energy from wind, taking advantage of local air circulation pattern driven by sunlight. Ocean thermal and ocean wave power plants use the sun's energy, as do solar cells and solar thermal collectors.
>
> M.A.K. Lodhi, *International Journal of Hydrogen Energy*, 2004.

## Renewables Need Political and Public Support

Renewables have largely sat on the sidelines, due to concerns from the industry that wind and solar do not (yet) dominate world energy supply, and the installed capacity of turbines and panels has trouble meeting current demand, let alone trying to fulfill what may become an insatiable future appetite for hydrogen. Get firmly established in mainstream utilities, the argument goes, before getting distracted by other markets, even if they are potentially more lucrative.

[*Refocus* magazine] has previously countered by suggesting that 'anything is possible' if there is the political and social will to grab the brass ring, noting the aggressive green targets in a growing number of countries, as well as campaigns such as the U.S. Apollo Alliance that wants to replicate the national determination which propelled that country's space program.

As in many areas, timing is everything in energy. The strong determination by some to transform world energy into a global hydrogen market has been overwhelming and has captured the public imagination, to the point where many niggling details have been overlooked. Perhaps this U.S. report will cause the juggernaut to be more closely examined, and give renewable energy an opportunity to regroup and seize the agenda.

*Rows of turbines like these could generate energy to make hydrogen and to help fuel America's conversion to a hydrogen economy.*

The NRC report examines reforming of natural gas, conversion of coal and use of nuclear to produce hydrogen, as well as the use of wind, biomass and solar.

"Of all renewable energy sources, using wind-turbine-generated electricity to electrolyze water, particularly in the near to medium term, has arguably the greatest potential for producing pollution-free hydrogen," but it says further cost reductions in turbine technology and generation are needed, as well as optimization of turbine-electrolyzers with hydrogen storage.

Wind energy for hydrogen production does not appear in the plan of the Department of Energy (DoE), but such systems "need to be an important element in DoE's hydrogen program, and need to be integrated into the hydrogen production strategy." Government should work with industry to develop wind systems that will be ready for deployment as the hydrogen infrastructure begins to develop, and it says the role of wind turbines must be "integrated into future hydrogen production strategies so that potential synergies can be better understood and utilized.". . .

"Because of the large volume of hydrogen potentially available from solar energy and its carbon dioxide–free hydrogen, multiple paths of development should be pursued until a clear winning technology emerges for hydrogen production," it adds. To address the hurdles facing hydrogen production, distribution and use, DoE should "shift its resources and attention" from development to more exploratory work, with more research into the area of using renewables for hydrogen production.

Although the National Research Council is a private institution, it provides advice to government under a congressional charter, and the study was sponsored by the Department of Energy. Members of the committee came from Princeton and Stanford universities, as well as MIT [Massachusetts Institute of Technology], Natural Resources Defense Council and others.

Whether that is sufficient credibility to change the course of the hydrogen transition remains to be seen, but the U.S. and global renewable energy community would do well to seize any delay in the evolution, and ensure that its technologies are fully and properly integrated into plans for the future.

# The Hydrogen Economy Is Nearly Here

## Wayne A. English

In the following article Wayne A. English claims that the United States will convert to a hydrogen economy soon. English points out that hydrogen fuel cells are already used in automobiles and that advances in hydrogen production and delivery are occurring rapidly. However, the true test of the potential of a hydrogen economy will come when utility companies adapt the technology to produce power for homes and businesses. English states that today's utility companies are likely to join the hydrogen trend since they already own the infrastructure to deliver energy and have experience in providing energy services to their customers. Wayne A. English has worked in the field of electricity distribution, nuclear engineering, and information technology since the 1970s.

With the advent of world wide terrorism, oil independence is a matter of domestic security. A side effect may be the end of electric utilities as we know them. For the United States and other oil-dependent economies to migrate to hydrogen-fueled automobiles will require wide-scale hydrogen production and distribution capability. That is so obvious that it almost sounds silly, yet it is that very production and distribution capability that may have far-reaching effects on utilities and their customers. Hydrogen technologies can

Wayne A. English, "Are Electric Utilities Obsolete?" *The Futurist*, March/April 2005, pp. 16–18. Reproduced by permission of The World Future Society.

power a cell phone, automobile, truck, railroad locomotive, house, commercial building, or factory. Further, unlike current electrical systems, hydrogen need not be used in real time. This means that hydrogen can be produced and accumulated for later use.

## Near-Term Markets and Plans

Hydrogen technologies will provide oil independence for our vehicles in the next 20 or 30 years. The U.S. government is facilitating the transition to hydrogen through such programs as the 21st Century Truck Partnership, the FreedomCAR (Cooperative Automotive Research) and Fuel Partnership, and other programs under the Department of Defense and the Department of Energy.

*Bill Reinert, national manager of Toyota's advanced technologies group, shows where hydrogen fuel is loaded into one of the automaker's hydrogen fuel cell vehicles.*

# California Hydrogen and Fuel Cell Activity

**OR**

**ID**

**NV**

Legend:
- ● Stationary Fuel Cell Installations
- ▢ Hydrogen Fueling Facilities
- 🎓 University/Research

Arcata

Herlong

West Sacramento
Davis
Sacramento
Richmond
Berkeley
Presidio
San Ramon
San Francisco
Yosemite
Livermore
Fresno

**CA**

Lompoc
Santa Barbara
Calabasas
Palmdale
CalTech
Port Hueneme
LADWP
Thousand Palms
Torrance
Riverside
Buena Park
Oceanside
Anaheim
San Diego
Irvine
Chula Vista

**AZ**

Source: California Air Resources Board, *California Hydrogen and Fuel Cell Guide*, 2004.

Many automakers are currently operating experimental fuel cell–powered cars. Also, existing internal combustion engines can be fueled by hydrogen with an increase in efficiency of roughly 25% over gasoline and a reduction of tailpipe emissions.

As we migrate to hydrogen, these vehicles and the hydrogen supply will support each other hand in glove, creating each other's market. The production and distribution capability of hydrogen on a massive scale will fuel a national distributed generation electrical system, in which electricity consumers, who are generating their own electricity using hydrogen, send their surplus electrical power back into the power grid.

Fuel cells and microturbines are capable of providing electrical power to far more than cars alone. In fact, anything that is now powered by electricity can be powered by hydrogen-electric technology. Power is power. Among the projects now under way [is] the U.S. Defense Department's installation of a one-megawatt (1341 horsepower) fuel cell into a 102 metric ton railroad locomotive. Caterpillar and FuelCell Energy are developing ultra-low emission electric generating products for industrial and commercial use. And Toshiba is developing a fuel cell to power laptop computers. Hydrogen-electric technology and the era of self-powered machines are dawning.

## Fuel Cell Competitiveness

Today's centralized electricity generation-transmission-distribution system was designed by Edison in the nineteenth century and is antiquated. There is no better demonstration of this than the blackout of August 2003 that plunged parts of the northeastern United States and Canada into darkness. The experts agree that one of the contributing factors was the age of the system. The energy industry has called for spending as much as $450 billion on infrastructure improvements. The money will be spent—that is not an issue. The question is whether we spend it on an antiquated nineteenth-century system or on twenty-first-century hydrogen technologies.

Fuel cells for residential markets will generate electricity at a cost competitive with power purchased from the electric grid in regions with high electric rates. The high cost of electricity in the northeast will likely make fuel cells a cost-competitive option for on-site power production. This, of course, will depend on the retail cost of hydrogen. But there, too, is danger, for to charge too high a price for hydrogen will only drive people and corporations to produce their own. Therefore, it is likely that fuel cells will be a widely available option for commercial applications in the next several years.

## Utilities in Transition

We think of electricity as a single source entity. Almost all customers have a single connection to the utility. Interrupt that connection and the customer is out of power. In the world of hydrogen, that will change.

Consider a small office building of three floors, each floor [requiring] 100kW [kilowatts] of electric power for a total of 300kW. You would think that a single 300kW fuel cell is the way to go, or perhaps one 100kW fuel cell on each floor, but let's not do that. Rather, let's install a 150kW fuel cell on each floor, for a total capacity of 450kW. Why? What this provides is a system in which any one of our three fuel cells can be out of service, because of trouble or maintenance, and the entire energy needs of the building can still be met. No lost productivity. No downtime. No phone calls to the local utility asking when the power will be restored. Business and industry will be very interested in a system that offers uninterrupted power and includes protection from thunderstorms, downed trees, and the myriad other causes of outages.

Extend this situation to a factory where the machines are powered by a single-redundancy system, as in our office building example. We know from industrial customers that even a short interruption of several seconds can play havoc with computer-controlled machines, resulting in the loss of thousands of hard, bottom-line dollars. In today's high-technology manufacturing world, electrical outages are not taken lightly. In fact, electric utilities are considering offering Probabilistic Risk Assessment (PRA) studies in an effort to predict when outages are likely to occur. Offering PRA and other services will help electric utilities compete with hydrogen technologies as fuel cells threaten to take their customers.

It is likely that commercial and industrial users will be the first to embrace hydrogen. To predict penetration of the residential market is problematic because of differences in what people are willing to spend for electric generation at home. Fuel cells will most likely get their start in this market in new home construction, just as wall-to-wall carpeting did: by rolling the cost into the purchase price of the home and amortizing it over

*At a 2005 conference, Brigadier General Roger Nadeau of the U.S. Research, Development, and Engineering Command unveils the army's first hydrogen-powered truck.*

the life of the mortgage. When this begins, electric utilities will be faced with the loss of their residential customers.

All is not bleak for utilities. They can and will use hydrogen technology for producing additional capacity in substations and other locations close to customer needs. And customers may not want to provide their own emergency and maintenance services and so will farm this service out to utilities or private contractors. Either way, this will be a game in which electric utilities can

*Animal manure may be used to produce hydrogen. A methane digester (inset) converts manure into methane, which can be used as a source of energy.*

compete. This competition will not be against other utilities but against new technology. The ability for any utility to retain customers will be up for grabs. Until now, if one company lost a customer, another utility picked that customer up. That may no longer be the case. New world, new rules.

## Hydrogen Generation and Transportation

Where the hydrogen will come from to power a country the size of the United States is a valid question. There are two sources for hydrogen:

- The electrolysis of water by electricity, which separates water molecules into pure hydrogen and oxygen. An advantage to this technology is that it can be used almost anywhere.
- The reforming of the fossil fuels oil and natural gas. These contain hydrocarbon molecules, which consist of only hydrogen and carbon. A fuel processor, or reformer, can remove the hydrogen from the hydrocarbon molecules. The hydrogen is retained and the carbon is discarded. This reduces air pollution but does nothing to help solve the greenhouse gas problem, so this method may be only a temporary solution as we migrate to hydrogen.

The energy for these methods may come from nuclear power plants specifically designed for producing hydrogen and electricity. Also, clean coal technologies are a viable source of hydrogen. The energy companies have an advantage in that they have been supplying power in one form or another for a long time and have the infrastructure and experience to keep doing so. Whatever technology or technologies we choose to generate hydrogen, oil and coal will not be superseded anytime soon. To assume otherwise is naïve.

Renewable technologies to power hydrogen production include solar, wind, ocean wave, ocean current, animal manure, and algae. Cow manure is currently used in a methane digester to power the Haubenschild Farm near Princeton, Minnesota. Hog farms are good candidates for this as well. The price of hydrogen at the retail level will be the final arbiter as to which of these technologies become viable. Algae, for example, produces electricity at 31 cents per kilowatt hour. That is currently far too expensive, but further research could make this technology more competitive.

In the future, energy producers may be very different from those currently using coal, oil, and nuclear power. In fact, energy production may even become a cottage industry.

## Future Energy Corporations

Ocean front property may soon be in a corporation's portfolio—not as a vacation spot but for energy generation. Hydrogen has one significant advantage over utility-supplied electric power—hydrogen need not be used in real time. It can be produced in an around-the-clock operation and stored, while electric power cannot.

At the seashore, there will be a wind farm and solar photovoltaic [light generating an electric current] cells. In the surf, there will be a wave generator. And offshore, perhaps in the Gulf Stream, there will be an ocean current generator. All of these technologies will generate electricity—some only when the wind blows or the sun shines, while others will generate virtually continuously. All will make electric power to crack water into hydrogen and oxygen. For those corporations where ocean front property is not appropriate, biomass or animal manure may be used, as is done at the Haubenschild Farm.

What you do not hear about in most discussions of hydrogen production is the commercially viable byproduct oxygen, which has medical, industrial, and military uses. The hydrogen, of course, will be used in fuel cells or microturbines for heating or cooling buildings and powering vehicles, laptops, cell phones, and personal digital assistants—all for the cost of the installed equipment amortized over time, tax deducted, and depreciated.

Depending on how well they anticipate the challenges ahead, electric utilities over the next 20–30 years will be either blessed or cursed to "live in interesting times."

# The Hydrogen Economy Is Far Off

## Robert F. Service

In the following article Robert F. Service claims that many
scientists have grave doubts about the feasibility of a hydrogen economy. Among these concerns are the high price of
hydrogen fuel, the inefficient ways in which it is produced,
the lack of infrastructure to distribute the fuel, and the large
amounts of energy required to create, store, and disseminate
hydrogen. Overcoming these obstacles will be difficult,
Service argues. He writes that several energy officials believe
that the emphasis on hydrogen is misplaced and that a focus
on other renewable energy sources might be more beneficial
in addressing world energy concerns. For these reasons,
Service reports, the hoped-for hydrogen economy may be a
long way off. Robert F. Service is the Pacific Northwest
bureau writer for *Science* magazine.

The bet on the hydrogen economy is at best a long shot.
Recent reports from the U.S. National Academy of
Sciences (NAS) and the American Physical Society (APS) conclude that researchers face daunting challenges in finding ways to
produce and store hydrogen, convert it to electricity, supply it to
consumers, and overcome vexing safety concerns. Any of those
hurdles could block a broad-based changeover. Solving them
simultaneously is "a very tall order," says Mildred Dresselhaus, a
physicist at the Massachusetts Institute of Technology (MIT),
who has served on recent hydrogen review panels with the U.S.

Robert F. Service, "The Hydrogen Backlash," *Science*, vol. 305, August 13, 2004.
Copyright © 2004 by AAAS. Reproduced by permission.

# It Takes Energy to Produce Hydrogen

To make $H_2$, the usable form of hydrogen, another energy source must be used, which costs energy and money.

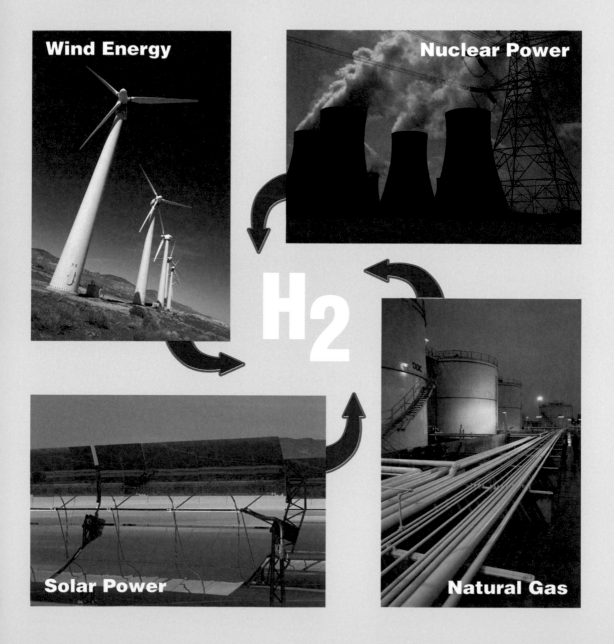

**Wind Energy**

**Nuclear Power**

**H₂**

**Solar Power**

**Natural Gas**

Department of Energy (DOE) and APS as well as serving as a reviewer for the related NAS report.

As a result, the transition to a hydrogen economy, if it comes at all, won't happen soon. "It's very, very far away from substantial deployed impact," says Ernest Moniz, a physicist at MIT and a former undersecretary of energy at DOE. "Let's just say decades, and I don't mean one or two."

In the meantime, some energy researchers complain that, by skewing research toward costly large-scale demonstrations of technology well before it's ready for market, governments risk repeating a pattern that has sunk previous technologies such as synfuels [synthetic fuels] in the 1980s. By focusing research on technologies that aren't likely to have a measurable impact until the second half of the century, the current hydrogen push fails to address the growing threat from greenhouse gas emissions from fossil fuels. "There is starting to be some backlash on the hydrogen economy," says Howard Herzog, an MIT chemical engineer. "The hype has been way overblown. It's just not thought through."

## Is Hydrogen the Perfect Alternative Fuel?

Almost everyone agrees that producing a viable hydrogen economy is a worthy long-term goal. For starters, worldwide oil production is expected to peak within the next few decades, and although supplies will remain plentiful long afterward, oil prices are expected to soar as international markets view the fuel as increasingly scarce. Natural gas production is likely to peak a couple of decades after oil. Coal, tar sands, and other fossil fuels should remain plentiful for at least another century. But these dirtier fuels carry a steep environmental cost: Generating electricity from coal instead of natural gas, for example, releases twice as much carbon dioxide ($CO_2$). And in order to power vehicles, they must be converted to a liquid or gas, which requires energy and therefore raises their cost.

Even with plenty of fossil fuels available, it's doubtful we'll want to use them all. Burning fossil fuels has already increased the concentration of $CO_2$ in the atmosphere from 280 to 370 parts per million (ppm) over the past 150 years. Unchecked, it's expected to pass 550 ppm this century, according to New York University physicist Martin Hoffert and colleagues in a [November] 2002 *Science* paper. "If sustained, [it] could eventually produce global warming comparable in magnitude but opposite in sign to the global cooling of the last Ice Age," the authors write. Development and population growth can only aggravate the problems.

On the face of it, hydrogen seems like the perfect alternative. When burned, or oxidized in a fuel cell, it emits no pollution, including no greenhouse gases. Gram for gram, it releases more energy than any other fuel. And as a constituent of water, hydrogen is all around us. No wonder it's being touted as the clean fuel of the future and the answer to modern society's addiction to fossil fuels. In April 2003, *Wired* magazine laid out "How Hydrogen Can Save America." Environmental gadfly Jeremy Rifkin has hailed the hydrogen economy as the next great economic revolution. And General Motors has announced plans to be the first company to sell 1 million hydrogen fuel cell cars by the middle of the next decade.

[In 2003], the Bush Administration plunged in, launching a 5-year, $1.7 billion initiative to commercialize hydrogen-powered cars by 2020. In March, the European Commission launched the first phase of an expected 10-year, €2.8 billion public-private partnership to develop hydrogen fuel cells. Last year, the Japanese government nearly doubled its fuel cell R&D budget to $268 million. Canada, China, and other countries have mounted efforts of their own. Car companies have already spent billions of dollars trying to reinvent their wheels—or at least their engines—to run on hydrogen: They've turned out nearly 70 prototype cars and trucks as well as dozens of buses. Energy and car companies have added scores of hydrogen fueling stations worldwide, with many more on the drawing boards. And the effort is still gaining steam.

## The Problem of Price

Still, despite worthwhile goals and good intentions, many researchers and energy experts say current hydrogen programs fall pitifully short of what's needed to bring a hydrogen economy to pass. The world's energy infrastructure is too vast, they say, and the challenges of making hydrogen technology competitive with fossil fuels too daunting unless substantially more funds are added to the pot. The current initiatives are just "a start," Dresselhaus says. "None of the reports say it's impossible," she adds. However, Dresselhaus says, "the problem is very difficult no matter how you slice it."

Economic and political difficulties abound, but the most glaring barriers are technical. At the top of the list: finding a simple and cheap way to produce hydrogen. As is often pointed out, hydrogen is not a fuel in itself, as oil and coal are. Rather, like electricity, it's an energy carrier that must be generated using another source of power. Hydrogen is the most common element in the universe. But on Earth, nearly all of it is bound to other elements in molecules, such as hydrocarbons and water. Hydrogen atoms must be split off these molecules to generate dihydrogen gas ($H_2$), the form it needs to be in to work in most fuel cells. These devices then combine hydrogen and oxygen to make water and liberate electricity in the process. But every time a fuel is converted from one source, such as oil, to another, such as electricity or hydrogen, it costs energy and therefore money.

Today, by far the cheapest way to produce hydrogen is by using steam and catalysts to break down natural gas into $H_2$ and $CO_2$. But although the technology has been around for decades, current steam reformers are only 85% efficient, meaning that 15% of the energy in natural gas is lost as waste heat during the reforming process. The upshot, according to Peter Devlin, who runs a hydrogen production program at DOE, is that it costs \$5 to produce the amount of hydrogen that releases as much energy as a gallon of gasoline. Current techniques for liberating hydrogen from coal, oil, or water are even less efficient. Renewable energy such as solar and wind power can also supply electricity to split water, without generating $CO_2$. But those technologies are even more expensive. . . .

## ANOTHER OPINION

### The Properties of Hydrogen Gas Make It Problematic

We have to accept that hydrogen is the lightest element and its physical properties do not suit the requirements of the energy market. The production, packaging, storage, transfer and delivery of the gas are so energy consuming that other solutions must be considered.

Ulf Bossel, *European Fuel Cell News*, July 2003.

## Storage Problems

If producing hydrogen cheaply has researchers scratching their heads, storing enough of it on board a car has them positively stymied. Because hydrogen is the lightest element, far less of it can fit into a given volume than other fuels. At room temperature and pressure, hydrogen takes up roughly 3000 times as much space as gasoline containing the same amount of energy. That means storing enough of it in a fuel tank to drive 300 miles (483 kilome-

*A test car is filled with hydrogen fuel at a solar hydrogen facility in Germany. Solar panels power the process that creates the hydrogen stored in the tall cylinder to the right.*

ters)—DOE's benchmark—requires either compressing it, liquefying it, or using some other form of advanced storage system.

Unfortunately, none of these solutions is up to the task of carrying a vehicle 300 miles on a tank. Nearly all of today's prototype hydrogen vehicles use compressed gas. But these are still bulky. Tanks pressurized to 10,000 pounds per square inch . . . take up to eight times the volume of a current gas tank to store the equivalent amount of fuel. Because fuel cells are twice as efficient as gasoline internal combustion engines, they need fuel tanks four times as large to propel a car the same distance.

Liquid hydrogen takes up much less room but poses other problems. The gas liquefies at -253°C, just a few degrees above absolute zero. Chilling it to that temperature requires about 30% of the energy in the hydrogen. And the heavily insulated tanks needed to keep liquid fuel from boiling away are still larger than ordinary gasoline tanks.

Other advanced materials are also being investigated to store hydrogen, such as carbon nanotubes, metal hydrides, and substances such as sodium borohydride that produce hydrogen by means of a chemical reaction. Each material has shown some promise. But for now, each still has fatal drawbacks, such as requiring high temperature or pressures, releasing the hydrogen too slowly, or requiring complex and time-consuming materials recycling. As a result, many experts are pessimistic. A report last year from DOE's Basic Energy Sciences Advisory Committee concluded: "A new paradigm is required for the development of hydrogen storage materials to facilitate a hydrogen economy." Peter Eisenberger, vice provost of Columbia University's Earth Institute, who chaired the APS report, is even more blunt. "Hydrogen storage is a potential showstopper," he says.

## Fuel Cell Breakthroughs Needed

Another area in need of serious progress is the fuel cells that convert hydrogen to electricity. Fuel cells have been around since the 1800s and have been used successfully for decades to power spacecraft. But their high cost and other drawbacks have kept them from being used for everyday applications such as cars. Internal combustion engines typically cost $30 for each kilowatt of power they produce. Fuel cells, which are loaded with precious-metal catalysts, are 100 times more expensive than that.

If progress on renewable technologies is any indication, near-term prospects for cheap fuel cells aren't bright, says Joseph Romm, former acting assistant secretary of energy for renewable energy in the Clinton Administration and author of a recent book, *The Hype About Hydrogen: Fact and Fiction in the Race to Save the Climate*. "It has taken wind power and solar power each about twenty years to see a tenfold decline in prices, after major government and private sector investments, and they still each comprise well under 1% of U.S. electricity generation," Romm said in written testimony in March before the House Science Committee reviewing the Administration's hydrogen initiative. "A major technology breakthrough is needed in transportation fuel cells before they will be practical." Various technical challenges—such as making fuel cells rugged enough to withstand the shocks of driving and ensuring the safety of cars loaded with flammable hydrogen gas—are also likely to make hydrogen cars costlier to engineer and slower to win public acceptance.

If they clear their internal technical hurdles, hydrogen fuel cell cars face an obstacle from outside: the infrastructure they need to refuel. If hydrogen is generated in centralized plants, it will have to be trucked or piped to its final destination. But because of hydrogen's low density, it would take 21 tanker trucks to haul the amount of energy a single gasoline truck delivers today, according to a study by Switzerland-based energy researchers Baldur Eliasson and Ulf Bossel. A hydrogen tanker traveling 500 kilometers would devour the equivalent of 40% of its cargo.

Ship the hydrogen as a liquid? Commercial-scale coolers are too energy-intensive for the job, Eliasson and Bossel point out. Transporting hydrogen through long-distance pipelines wouldn't improve matters much. Eliasson and Bossel calculate that 1.4% of the hydrogen flowing through a pipeline would be required to power the compressors needed to pump it for every 150 kilometers the gas must travel. The upshot, Eliasson and Bossel report: "Only 60% to 70% of the hydrogen fed into a pipeline in Northern Africa would actually arrive in Europe."

To lower those energy penalties, some analysts favor making hydrogen at fueling stations or in homes where it will be used, with equipment powered by the existing electricity grid or natural gas. But onsite production wouldn't be cheap, either. Eliasson and Bossel calculate that to supply hydrogen for 100 to 2000 cars per day, an electrolysis-based fueling station would require between 5 and 81 megawatts of electricity. "The generation of hydrogen at filling stations would make a threefold increase of electric power generating capacity necessary," they report. And at least for the foreseeable future, that extra electricity is likely to come from fossil fuels.

Whichever approach wins out, it will need a massive new hydrogen infrastructure to deliver the goods. The 9 million tons of hydrogen (enough to power between 20 million and 30 million

*Before fuel cells can be widely marketable, they must overcome their performance problems and high cost.*

cars) that the United States produces yearly for use in gasoline refining and chemical plants pale beside the needs of a full-blown transportation sector. For a hydrogen economy to catch on, the fuel must be available in 30% to 50% of filling stations when mass-market hydrogen cars become available, says Bernard Bulkin, former chief scientist at BE. A recent study by Marianne Mintz and colleagues at Argonne National Laboratory in Illinois found that creating the infrastructure needed to fuel 40% of America's cars would cost a staggering $500 billion or more.

Energy and car companies are unlikely to spend such sums unless they know mass-produced hydrogen vehicles are on the way. Carmakers, however, are unlikely to build fleets of hydrogen vehicles without stations to refuel them. "We face a 'chicken and egg' problem that will be difficult to overcome," said Michael Ramage,

Arnie Glick. Reproduced by permission.

a former executive vice president of ExxonMobil Research and Engineering, who chaired the NAS hydrogen report, when the report was released in February.

## Where to Focus?

Each of the problems faced by the hydrogen economy—production, storage, fuel cells, safety, and infrastructure—would be thorny enough on its own. For a hydrogen economy to succeed, however, all of these challenges must be solved simultaneously. One loose end and the entire enterprise could unravel. Because many of the solutions require fundamental breakthroughs, many U.S. researchers question their country's early heavy emphasis on expensive demonstration projects of fuel cell cars, fueling stations, and other technologies.

# The U.S. Government's Plan to Adopt a Hydrogen Economy

### U.S. Department of Energy

In February 2004 the U.S. Department of Energy (DOE) released its *Hydrogen Posture Plan* to illustrate America's readiness to advance toward a hydrogen economy. According to the plan, excerpted in the following selection, the United States will likely make the conversion to hydrogen fuel sometime around 2030. The DOE is optimistic that scientists and engineers will find ways to make hydrogen affordable and accessible for homes and businesses in coming years. The result will be a full-fledged hydrogen economy sometime before midcentury.

Although hydrogen is the most abundant element in the universe, it must be produced from other hydrogen-containing compounds such as fossil fuels, biomass, or water. Each method of production requires a source of energy, i.e., thermal (heat), electrolytic (electricity), or photolytic (light) energy. Hydrogen is either consumed on site or distributed to end users via pipelines, trucks, or other means. Hydrogen can be stored as a liquid, gas, or chemical compound and is converted into energy through fuel cells or by combustion in turbines and engines. Fuel cells now in development will not only provide a new way to produce power, but will also improve energy conversion efficiency, especially in transportation applications.

U.S. Department of Energy, *Hydrogen Posture Plan: An Integrated Research, Development, and Demonstration Plan.* Washington, DC: 2004. Reproduced by permission.

The U.S. chemical and refining industries have a limited number of commercial facilities in place for the production and delivery of hydrogen (about nine million tons is manufactured annually for use in these industries). Those operations are localized, and cannot provide the technology advances and carbon management required for widespread use of hydrogen in the energy sector (i.e., large-scale, low-cost production methods, and storage and delivery infrastructures compatible with automotive and distributed generation applications). Currently, technical challenges remain (centered around cost, performance, and safety) in the elements of the hydrogen energy infrastructure. . . . Addressing these challenges will require a coordinated, multi-agency effort. . . .

## Long-Term Vision of the Hydrogen Economy

In the long-term vision of the hydrogen economy (which will take several decades to achieve), hydrogen will be available in all regions of the country and will serve all sectors of the economy. It will be produced from fossil fuels (with carbon capture and sequestration [to eliminate the release of greenhouse gases into the atmosphere]), renewable energy, and nuclear energy. It will be used throughout the transportation, electric power, and consumer sectors. Hydrogen will be produced in centralized facilities, in distributed facilities at power parks, fueling stations, rural areas, and community locations. Hydrogen production and storage costs will be competitive; the basic components of a national hydrogen delivery and distribution network will be in place; and hydrogen-powered fuel cells, engines, and turbines will have become mature technologies in mass production for use in cars, homes, offices, and factories.

Hydrogen will be the dominant fuel for government and transit bus fleets. It will be used in personal vehicles and light duty trucks. Hydrogen will be combusted directly in turbines and reciprocating engines to generate electricity and thermal energy for homes, offices, and factories. It will be used in fuel cells for both mobile and stationary applications. U.S. companies that commercialize hydrogen technologies will be exporting products and services around the world. Developing countries will have access to clean, sustainable, economical hydrogen-based energy systems to meet their growing energy demands.

## Getting from Here to There

Achieving this vision will require a combination of technological breakthroughs, market acceptance, and large investments in a national hydrogen energy infrastructure. Success will not happen overnight, or even over years, but rather over decades; it will require an evolutionary process that phases hydrogen in as the technologies and their markets are ready. . . .

In the near- to mid-term, most hydrogen will likely be produced by technologies that do not require a new hydrogen delivery infrastructure—i.e., from distributed natural gas and electrolysis of water using electricity (with emphasis on renewable sources such as wind power). As research, development and demonstration (RD&D) efforts progress along renewable, nuclear, and clean coal and natural gas production pathways, a suite of technologies will become available in the mid- and longer-term to produce hydrogen from a diverse array of domestic resources. The economic viability of these different production pathways will be strongly affected by regional factors, such as feedstock availability and cost, delivery approaches, and regulatory environment.

For hydrogen to become a viable fuel source, advanced hydrogen storage technologies will also be required, especially for automotive applications. Current storage systems are too heavy, too large, and too costly. Technologies to convert hydrogen into useful energy—fuel cells and combustion technologies—must be further improved to lower cost and improve performance. Finally, the infrastructure to deliver hydrogen where it is needed must be developed and constructed. The

*A hydrogen-powered patrol car is open for viewing at the National Hydrogen Association 2006 convention in Los Angeles.*

hydrogen infrastructure can evolve along with the conversion and production technologies, since most of the infrastructure that is developed for fossil-based hydrogen will also be applicable to renewable- and nuclear-based hydrogen. Infrastructure will begin with pilot projects and expand to local, regional, and ultimately national and international applications. More detailed economic analyses of the different production, storage, conversion and distribution options will also be essential. . . .

A full transition to a hydrogen-based energy system will take several decades and require strong public and private parternship. In Phase I, government and private organizations will research, develop, and demonstrate "critical path" technologies and safety assurance prior to investing heavily in infrastructure. Public education and codes and standards must be developed concurrently with the RD&D. The President's Hydrogen Fuel Initiative is consistent with completion of the critical path technology RD&D phase leading up to a commercialization decision in 2015. This Phase could continue beyond 2015 to support basic science and to further develop advanced, sustainable technologies for hydrogen production and use. The commercialization decision criteria will be based on the ability of hydrogen fuel technology to meet customer requirements and to establish the business case.

Phase II, Transition to the Marketplace [ca. 2010–2030], begins as industries begin to manufacture and market hydrogen (using

## A Time Line for America's Transition to a Hydrogen Economy

### 2000–2010

- Use hydrogen to power the space shuttle
- Use hydrogen for portable power
- Use hydrogen to power the U.S. government's vehicles

### 2010–2020

- Use hydrogen to power military vehicles
- Use hydrogen to power bus fleets

### 2020–2030

- Use hydrogen to power commercial fleets
- Introduce hydrogen-powered vehicles for consumer use

### 2030–2040

- Use hydrogen to power homes and businesses via utility companies

Source: U.S. Department of Energy, www.eere.energy.gov, 2004.

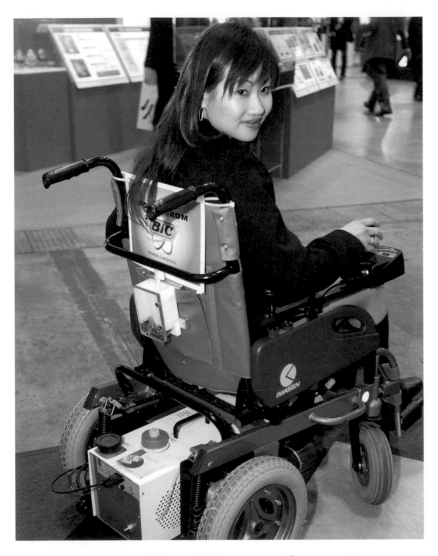

*A representative of Japan's Sumitomo Corporation
demonstrates a wheelchair powered by a fuel cell at the
2005 International Fuel Cell Expo.*

the existing natural gas and electric grid infrastructure) and fuel
cell technologies in portable, stationary, and transportation applications. Consumers will need compelling reasons to purchase
these products; public benefits such as high efficiency and low
emissions are not enough. The all-electronic car powered by

*The General Motors Hy-wire does not have a bulky internal combustion engine. It runs entirely off a hydrogen fuel cell that powers a relatively small electric motor.*

hydrogen fuel cells (such as the General Motors Hy-wire) is one example of value delivery; it offers the consumer much improved performance through elimination of mechanical parts and greater design flexibility [through interchangeable body design]. During this phase, government agencies will work to develop codes and standards required for the transition. Government and industry involvement continue as hydrogen-related technologies meet or exceed customer requirements.

As these markets become established, government can foster their further growth by playing the role of "early adopter" and by creating policies that stimulate the market. Phase III, Expansion of Markets and Infrastructure, proceeds if industry makes a positive commercialization decision in 2015 [and may last until 2035]. During this phase the business case for a hydrogen-based economy is realized, attracting investment in infrastructure, for fuel cell manufacturing and hydrogen production and delivery. Government policies still may be required to nurture this infrastructure expansion phase. Phase IV, several decades from now [ca. 2025 and beyond], is Realization of the Hydrogen Vision, when consumer requirements will be met or exceeded, national benefits in terms of energy security and improved environmental quality are achieved, and industry can receive adequate return on investment and compete globally.

# Facts About Hydrogen

## Properties of the Element Hydrogen
- Chemical symbol: H
- Atomic weight: 1.00797
- Density: 0.071 g/ml
- Boiling point: -252.87°C
- Hydrogen is the most abundant element in the universe, making up about 90 percent of all matter. It is the third most abundant element on Earth, where it is primarily bound up in water ($H_2O$) and organic matter.

## Properties of Hydrogen Fuel
- Liquid hydrogen has a density of 0.07 grams/cubic centimeter; in comparison with gasoline (0.75g/cc), liquid hydrogen contains about 2.6 times the energy per unit mass as gasoline but requires about four times the volume per unit energy. Thus a tank of hydrogen would require four times the volume of a comparable gasoline tank, but the hydrogen fuel would weigh significantly less than the gasoline.
- When burned as a fuel, hydrogen is nonpolluting because it emits only water vapor and heat. Many processes to turn hydrogen into a fuel, however, require the burning of fossil fuels, which emit polluting greenhouse gases.

## Methods of Hydrogen Fuel Production
*Thermochemical*
- Steam reformation using natural gas, coal, methanol, or gasoline. In the United States, 95 percent of hydrogen is produced by steam reforming.
- Gasification or pyrolysis of biomass, from which hydrogen can be reformed.

*Electrochemical*
- Using an electric current to separate hydrogen out of water.

*Photoelectrochemical*
- Splitting water by directing sunlight toward a semiconductor immersed in water.

*Photobiological*
- Using the natural photosynthetic processes of bacteria or algae to produce hydrogen.

## Hydrogen Production Statistics

- According to the Department of Energy 9 million tons of hydrogen are produced in the United States each year. That is enough to power 20 to 30 million automobiles or 5 to 8 million homes. About 17 percent of the hydrogen produced is for commercial sale.
- About eighty plants in the United States are devoted to producing hydrogen.
- Most hydrogen produced in the United States is used by industry in refining, treating metals, and food processing. The National Aeronautics and Space Administration (NASA) uses hydrogen as a primary fuel for space shuttles and to run shipboard electrical systems.
- Worldwide, 48 percent of hydrogen is produced from natural gas, 30 percent from oil, 18 percent from coal, and 4 percent from water electrolysis.
- Hydrogen costs about $0.32 per pound if used at the site where it is produced. Transporting hydrogen for use can increase the cost to between $1.00 and $1.40 per pound.

## Hydrogen Infrastructure

- In the United States, three hydrogen producers—Air Liquide Group, Air Products and Chemicals Inc., and Praxair Inc.—operate hydrogen pipelines in California, Indiana, Louisiana, and Texas. The pipelines are short and serve a small customer base.
- Hydrogen is also delivered by tanker trucks. It is usually liquefied for transport and then vaporized at its destination site.

Eleven North American plants have the capacity to produce 283 tons of liquid hydrogen per day.

- There are twenty-five hydrogen refueling stations in the United States (sixteen in California, three in Michigan, two in Arizona, one each in the District of Columbia, Nevada, North Carolina, and Pennsylvania). Only a few allow public access. Other countries with hydrogen refueling stations are Australia (one), Belgium (two), Canada (six), China (Hong Kong) (one), Denmark (one), Germany (nine), Iceland (one), India (one), Italy (one), Japan (eleven), Luxembourg (one), Portugal (two), South Korea (one), Spain (two), and Sweden (one).

## Types of Fuel Cells

*Alkaline Fuel Cells*

- The alkaline fuel cell uses an alkaline electrolyte such as potassium hydroxide and various metals as catalysts for its electrodes. Originaly used by NASA on space missions, alkaline fuel cells are now being used in hydrogen-powered vehicles.
- Operating temperature: 90–100°C
- Energy efficiency: 45–60 percent
- Electrical power: less than 20 kilowatts (kW)

*Direct Methanol Fuel Cells*

- Direct methanol fuel cells (DMFC) use methanol instead of hydrogen as their fuel. These fuel cells are similar to the polymer electrolyte membrane (PEM) variety in that they use a polymer membrane as an electrolyte. However, a catalyst on the DMFC anode draws hydrogen from liquid methanol, eliminating the need for a fuel reformer.
- Operating temperature: 60–130°C
- Energy efficiency: 40 percent
- Electrical power: less than 10kW

*Molten Carbonate Fuel Cells*

- Molten carbonate fuel cells (MCFC) use a molten carbonate salt as the electrolyte. They can be fueled with coal-derived fuel gases or natural gas and are being developed for electrical utility, industrial, and military applications.

- Operating temperature: 600–1000°C
- Energy efficiency: 45–65 percent
- Electrical power: more than 1 megawatt (MW)

*Phosphoric Acid Fuel Cells*

- A phosphoric acid fuel cell (PAFC) consists of electrodes made of a platinum catalyst on carbon paper and a silicon carbide matrix that holds the phosphoric acid electrolyte. This is the most commercially developed type of fuel cell and is being used in hotels, hospitals, and office buildings. The PAFC can also be used in large vehicles, such as buses.
- Operating temperature: 175–200°C
- Energy efficiency: 36–38 percent
- Electrical power: more than 50 MW

*Polymer Electrolyte Membrane Fuel Cells*

- The polymer electrolyte membrane (PEM) fuel cell (also called a proton exchange membrane fuel cell) uses a solid polymer as an electrolyte and carbon electrodes containing a platinum catalyst. Because they are lightweight and generate high power, PEM cells appear to be more adaptable to automobile use than the PAFC. These cells operate at relatively low temperatures and can vary their output to meet shifting power demands. These cells are the best candidates for light-duty vehicles and for buildings.
- Operating temperature: 60–100°C
- Energy efficiency: 40–60 percent
- Electrical power: less than 250kW

*Solid Oxide Fuel Cells*

- Solid oxide fuel cells (SOFC) use a thin layer of zirconium oxide as a solid ceramic electrolyte and include a lanthanum manganate cathode and a nickel-zirconia anode. They are a promising option for applications requiring large amounts of power, such as industrial uses or central electricity-generating stations.
- Operating temperature: 600–1000°C
- Energy efficiency: 50–65 percent
- Electrical power: less than 1 MW

## Hybrid Car Statistics

*2006 Honda Civic Hybrid*
- 50 miles per gallon (mpg) (combined highway and city)
- 554 miles on one tank of gasoline
- Vehicle cost: $21,850 Manufacturers Suggested Retail Price

*2006 Honda Insight*
- automatic transmission: 56 mpg (combined)
- 534 miles on one tank of gasoline
- Vehicle cost: $21,530 MSRP

- manual transmission: 63 mpg (combined)
- 601 miles on one tank of gasoline
- Vehicle cost: $19,330 MSRP

*2006 Toyota Prius*
- 55 mpg (combined)
- 589 miles on one tank of gasoline
- Vehicle cost: $21,725 MSRP

# Glossary

**biomass:** Biological crops or wastes harvested as an energy source. Biomass is typically heated and then gasified to release a carbon-rich gas from which hydrogen can be extracted through a reformation process.

**carbon sequestration:** The capturing of carbon dioxide emissions from the burning of fossil fuels. Sequestration prevents the carbon dioxide (a greenhouse gas) from being released into the atmosphere. The captured gas could be stored or recycled for later use.

**catalyst:** A chemical agent that speeds up a reaction. Platinum is a common catalyst used to initiate the chemical processes within some fuel cells.

**electrode:** An electricity-conducting substance that is used to make contact with the nonmetallic part of an electric circuit (such as an electrolyte solution). Electrodes may be either anodes or cathodes. Anodes steer electrons out of the electrolyte part of an electric cell (battery) along a circuit path. Cathodes draw the electrons back into the cell.

**electrolysis:** Passing an electric current through water to separate out hydrogen gas and oxygen gas.

**electrolyzer:** A device in which electrolysis is performed. An electrolyzer has three constituent parts: an electrolyte solution (distilled water mixed with a salt, acid, or base), two electrodes (an anode and a cathode), and a separator (which keeps the electrodes apart yet allows electric current to pass through).

**Erren engine:** A type of internal combustion engine using hydrogen as the sole combustible fuel or as one of multiple combustible fuels. Erren engines were popular in Germany during the 1930s when their inventor, Rudolf Erren, was using them to power buses, trucks, and even submarines.

**fossil fuels:** Carbon-based energy sources such as coal and natural gas. The burning of fossil fuels typically emits environmentally harmful greenhouse gases.

**fuel cell:** A device in which hydrogen and oxygen are combined with the help of a catalyst. The results of the bonding reaction are water (vapor) and an electric current that can be used for power.

**gasification of coal:** The superheating of coal (to 900°C) until it turns into gaseous form. It is then combined with steam and a catalyst to produce hydrogen, with carbon monoxide and carbon dioxide as by-products.

**greenhouse gas:** Any of a number of gases that linger in the atmosphere, trapping heat. Carbon dioxide and methane are greenhouse gases commonly produced during the burning of fossil fuels for energy.

**hybrid vehicle:** An automobile that runs partly via a gasoline-powered internal combustion engine and partly via a hydrogen fuel cell.

**hydrides:** A chemical compound in which hydrogen is bonded to any other element. The term was once restricted to compounds containing metals (yielding the common series of compounds referred to as metal hydrides).

**hydrogen economy:** A term used to describe a local, national, or global society in which nonpolluting hydrogen and renewable resources have replaced fossil fuels as the main source of energy.

**internal combustion engine:** An engine that ignites explosive gases inside an internal chamber to provide force to propel a car or other machinery.

**photoelectrochemical (PEC) hydrogen production:** Using sunlight striking against a catalyst submerged or dissolved in water to produce an electric current. The current drives a water-splitting reaction (electrolysis) that produces hydrogen.

**photolytic hydrogen production:** Any method of producing hydrogen that uses sunlight to split water.

**polymer electrolyte membrane (PEM) fuel cell:** Also referred to as a proton exchange membrane fuel cell, a PEM fuel cell uses an electrolyte membrane to aid the process of combining hydrogen and oxygen fuels to produce an electric current. Current automobile hybrids use PEM fuel cells.

**power grid:** A network of power lines and power stations that conveys energy from a source (power plant) to a variety of destinations (including homes, businesses, and industries).

**pyrolysis:** The chemical decomposition of an organic substance under high pressure and heat without the use of oxygen.

**renewable energy sources:** Sources of energy that are not exhausted after use. Renewable energy sources include wind energy, solar energy, and hydro energy.

**semiconductor:** A material that conducts electricity better than an insulator (such as rubber) but not as well as a conductor (such as copper). Silicon is a common semiconductor.

**steam reformation:** One method of producing hydrogen, steam reformation is a process in which a hydrocarbon-rich fossil fuel (most commonly, natural gas) is reacted with steam over a catalytic surface. The reaction separates the hydrogen out of the fossil fuel and leaves carbon monoxide and carbon dioxide as by-products.

**thermolysis:** The decomposition of a substance through burning.

**watt:** A unit of power equal to one joule of energy per second. A kilowatt (kW) is one thousand watts. A megawatt (MW) is one million watts.

# Chronology

**1766**
British scientist Henry Cavendish identifies hydrogen ($H_2$) as a unique element (though he does not name it "hydrogen"). He would later show that hydrogen was one of two principal elements in water.

**1783**
French physicist Jacques Alexander Cesar Charles devises and pilots the first hydrogen-filled balloon.

**1788**
French chemist Antoine Lavoisier names hydrogen from the Greek words *hydro* (meaning "water") and *genes* (meaning "born of").

**1800**
British scientists William Nicholson and Sir Anthony Carlisle run an electric current through water and discover that the reaction splits the water molecules ($H_2O$) into hydrogen and oxygen gases. This process is later dubbed "electrolysis."

**1838**
Swiss chemist Christian Friedrich Schoenbein demonstrates that the forced combination of hydrogen and oxygen gases yields water and a small electric current. This principle is the basis of fuel cell technology.

**1845**
British scientist Sir William Grove employs Schoenbein's process to create the first working fuel cell.

**1874**
British author Jules Verne writes *The Mysterious Island*, a fictional work that contains a prophetic discussion about the use of hydrogen as an abundant energy alternative to coal.

**1923**
British scientist and author J.B.S. Haldane gives a lecture at

Cambridge University in which he predicts that in four hundred years wind power will be harnessed to produce hydrogen and oxygen through electrolysis. The gases, he states, will be stored in liquid form until needed to produce energy through their recombination.

## 1928

German engineer Rudolf Erren receives patents for various engines that run on pure hydrogen or a mixture of fuels. In the next decade, Erren convinces the Nazi German government to adopt some of his "Erren engines" for a fleet of industrial trucks, buses, and rail cars.

## 1937

The German airship *Hindenburg* bursts into flame on its descent over Lakewood, New Jersey. The hydrogen gas that filled the dirigible is initially thought to have caused the fire, but later evidence indicates that the hydrogen did not cause the accident. The crash of the *Hindenburg* convinces many people that hydrogen is too unsafe to have practical uses.

## 1959

British scientist Francis T. Bacon builds the first practical hydrogen-air fuel cell. Named the Bacon cell, the five-kilowatt system is used to power a welding machine. Bacon cells have since been used for daily energy needs on board National Aeronautics and Space Administration manned spacecraft. Later in 1959, Harry Karl Ihrig, an engineer for the Allis-Chalmers Manufacturing Company, demonstrates how a fifteen-kilowatt fuel cell could run a twenty-horsepower tractor. Ihrig's tractor is the first publicized fuel cell vehicle.

## 1970

Australian electrochemist and General Motors consultant John O'M. Bockris coins the term *hydrogen economy* during a discussion at the General Motors Technical Center in Warren, Michigan. He relates the event in his 1975 book, *Energy: The Solar-Hydrogen Alternative*, a work that describes the economic and environmental impact of creating a hydrogen-powered society. Also in 1970, Italian scientist Cesar Marchetti lectures at Cornell University on how hydrogen fuel—generated from water in nuclear reactors—could eliminate the world's dependence on fossil fuels.

## 1973
The Organization of Petroleum Exporting Countries' oil embargo and the attendant rising costs of gasoline renew interest in creating practical applications for hydrogen fuel and renewable energy sources.

## 1974
The Federal Hydrogen Research and Development Program becomes part of the U.S. Department of Energy. The Hydrogen Economy Miami Energy Conference (THEME) is the first international conference held to discuss hydrogen energy. Following the conference, several attending scientists and engineers form the International Association for Hydrogen Energy. The International Energy Agency (IEA) is established to conduct and fund hydrogen research in order to overcome the world's dependence on fossil fuels.

## 1988
American William Conrad becomes the first person to pilot an airplane powered by hydrogen fuel.

## 1989
Various industrial representatives, politicians, and scientists found the National Hydrogen Association to further practical hydrogen technology.

## 1990
The first solar-powered hydrogen production plant is opened at Solar-Wasserstoff-Bayern in southern Germany. The U.S. Congress passes the Spark M. Matsunaga Hydrogen Research, Development and Demonstration Act, which sets out a five-year management and implementation plan for hydrogen research and development in the United States. Later in the year, General Motors begins working on a proton exchange membrane (PEM) fuel cell for vehicles.

## 1997
After demonstrating its first electric fuel cell car in 1994, Daimler Benz partners with Ballard Power Systems to jointly

invest $300 million in fuel cell vehicle research and development.

### 1998
Working in cooperation with Daimler Benz and Ballard Power Systems, the government of Iceland announces that it aims to adopt a hydrogen economy by 2030.

### 1999
Royal Dutch/Shell Group, a major fuel supplier, establishes a hydrogen research division. The first three hydrogen fueling stations in the world are set up in Munich and Hamburg, Germany, and in Dearborn, Michigan.

### 2000
Ballard Power Systems displays the world's first production-ready PEM fuel cell for vehicles.

### 2003
U.S. president George W. Bush delivers a State of the Union address in which he promises to make America "less dependent on foreign sources of energy" by pledging $1.2 billion of federal funds to advance research and development of hydrogen fuel cells for automobiles.

### 2004
The U.S. Department of Energy's *Hydrogen Posture Plan* predicts that America will make a complete transition to a hydrogen economy between 2030 and 2040.

### 2005
Twenty-three U.S. states have adopted policies in support of a national transition to hydrogen fuel and fuel cells.

# For Further Reading

## Books and Papers

Busby, Rebecca L., *Hydrogen and Fuel Cells: A Comprehensive Guide*. Tulsa, OK: PennWell, 2005.

Dickson, Edward M., John W. Ryan, and Marilyn H. Smulyan, *The Hydrogen Energy Economy: A Realistic Appraisal of Prospects and Impacts*. New York: Praeger, 1977.

Dunn, Seth, "Hydrogen Futures: Toward a Sustainable Energy System," *Worldwatch Paper 157*. Washington, DC: Worldwatch Institute, 2001.

Haldane, J.B.S., *Daedalus, or Science and the Future*. London: Kegan Paul, Trench, Trubner, 1925.

Hoffmann, Peter, *The Forever Fuel: The Story of Hydrogen*. Boulder, CO: Westview, 1981.

————, *Tomorrow's Energy: Hydrogen, Fuel Cells, and the Prospects for a Cleaner Planet*. Cambridge, MA: MIT Press, 2001.

International Energy Agency, *Hydrogen and Fuel Cells: Review of National R & D Programs*. Paris: Organisation for Economic Co-operation and Development/International Energy Agency, 2004.

National Research Council and National Academy of Engineering, *The Hydrogen Economy: Opportunities, Costs, Barriers, and R & D Needs*. Washington, DC: National Academies Press, 2004.

Ogden, Joan M., and Robert H. Williams, *Solar Hydrogen: Moving Beyond Fossil Fuels*. Washington, DC: World Resources Institute, 1989.

Rifkin, Jeremy, *The Hydrogen Economy: The Creation of the World-Wide Energy Web and the Redistribution of Power on Earth*. New York: Jeremy P. Tarcher/Putnam, 2002.

Romm, Joseph J., *The Hype About Hydrogen: Fact and Fiction in the Race to Save the Climate*. Washington, DC: Island Press, 2004.

Sorenson, Bent, *Hydrogen and Fuel Cells: Emerging Technologies and Applications*. St. Louis: Academic Press, 2005.

Sperling, Daniel, and James S. Cannon, eds., *The Hydrogen Energy Transition: Moving Toward the Post-Petroleum Age in Transportation*. St. Louis: Academic Press, 2004.

Vaitheeswaran, Vijay V., *Power to the People: How the Coming Energy Revolution Will Transform an Industry, Change Our Lives, and Maybe Even Save the Planet*. New York: Farrar, Straus and Giroux, 2003.


## Periodicals

Arndt, Michael, "Where Our Energy Will Come From," *Business Week*, October 11, 2004.

Balat, Mustafa, and Nuray Ozdemir, "New and Renewable Hydrogen Production Processes," *Energy Sources*, October 2005.

Banerjee, Neela, and Danny Hakim, "U.S. Ends Car Plan on Gas Efficiency; Looks to Fuel Cells," *New York Times*, January 9, 2002.

Behar, Michael, "The Hydrogen Economy May Be More Distant than It Appears," *Popular Science*, January 2005.

Bertel, E., K.S. Lee, and C. Nordberg, "Nuclear Energy in the Hydrogen Economy," *NEA News*, 2004.

Brown, Kenneth, "Producing Renewable Hydrogen from Biomass," *BioCycle*, January 2004.

Doty, F. David, "Biofuels Versus Hydrogen," *Chemical & Engineering News*, March 14, 2005.

Dunlop, John, "Renewable Hydrogen Technologies: A Low-Cost Solar Solution to the Clean Hydrogen Problem," *Refocus*, January 2004.

Dunn, Seth, "Islands of Hope in Hydrogen," *New Internationalist*, December 2002.

Easterbrook, Gregg, "Car Talk," *New Republic*, February 24, 2003.

*Economist*, "Why the Future Is Hybrid," December 4, 2004.

Eggertson, Bill, "Seize the Agenda: Integrating Renewables into a Hydrogen Future," *Refocus*, March 2004.

Fahey, Jonathan, "Hydrogen Gas," *Forbes*, April 25, 2005.

Fishman, Ted C., "Cars That Guzzle Grass," *New York Times Magazine*, September 25, 2005.

Fonda, Daren, Steve Barnes, and Joseph Szczesny, "Make Vroom for the Hybrids," *Time*, May 24, 2004.

Gorman, Jessica, "Hydrogen: The Next Generation," *Science News*, October 12, 2002.

Gresser, Julian, and James A. Cusumano, "Hydrogen and the New Energy Economy," *Futurist*, March/April 2005.

Kolbert, Elizabeth, "The Car of Tomorrow," *New Yorker*, August 11, 2003.

Lodhi, M.A.K., "Helio-Hydro and Helio-Thermal Production of Hydrogen," *International Journal of Hydrogen Energy*, 2004.

Motavalli, Jim, "What a Gas! A Week in Suburbia with a Hydrogen Honda," *New York Times*, June 5, 2005.

Newman, Richard J., "A New Kind of Combustion in Detroit," *U.S. News & World Report*, May 9, 2005.

Olson, Robert L., "Hydrogen Develoment," *Current*, October 2003.

Petit, Charles W., "Yellow Light for a Green Fuel," *U.S. News & World Report*, December 22, 2003.

Port, Otis, "Hydrogen Cars Are Almost Here, But . . . ," *Business Week*, January 24, 2005.

Predd, Pachi Patel, "Cheaper Hydrogen Beckons," *IEEE Spectrum*, March 2005.

Randerson, James, "Hydrogen: Saviour or Fatal Distraction," *New Scientist*, August 21, 2004.

Reynolds, Kim, et al., "Hydrogen, Fuel Cells, and Reality," *Motor Trend*, August 2004.

Rifkin, Jeremy, "Hydrogen: Empowering the People," *Nation*, December 23, 2002.

Schnoor, Jerald L., "A Hydrogen-Fueled Economy?" *Environmental Science & Technology*, June 1, 2004.

Sperling, Daniel, and Joan Ogden, "The Hope for Hydrogen," *Issues in Science & Technology*, Spring 2004.

Venables, Mark, "China Stakes Its Future on Hydrogen," *IEEE Review*, May 2005.

Wald, Matthew L., "Hydrogen Production Method Could Bolster Fuel Supplies," *New York Times*, November 28, 2004.

————, "Questions About a Hydrogen Economy," *Scientific American*, May 2004.

## Web Sites

**California Fuel Cell Partnership** (www.fuelcellpartnership.org). Formed in 1999, the partnership is composed of government and business leaders with an interest in developing clean energy technologies. The Web site contains news items, an events calendar, and a resource center related to the state's accomplishments in experimental energy technologies.

**Fuel Cells 2000** (www.fuelcells.org). An outgrowth of the nonprofit Breakthrough Technologies Institute, this Web site contains information on fuel cells and their applications. The basics of fuel cell design and operation, as well as the generation and transport of hydrogen fuel, are explained on the site.

**Fuel Cell Today** (www.fuelcelltoday.com). This worldwide informational Web site is designed to accelerate the development and acceptance of fuel cells. The site compiles many news articles and event listings related to fuel cells.

**The Hydrogen and Fuel Cell Letter (HFCL)** (www.hfcletter.com). An online publication since 1986, the HFCL covers the business, science, economics, and politics of hydrogen. Many news items are archived on the site. The editor of the HFCL is Peter Hoffmann, a science and technology writer and the author of two popular books on hydrogen energy.

**National Hydrogen Association (NHA)** (www.hydrogenus.com). Formed by business and research groups in 1989, the NHA is an advocacy organization promoting the transition to a hydrogen economy. The NHA Web site has a number of fact sheets, press releases, and other informational resources on hydrogen power.

**U.S. Department of Energy** (www.eere.energy.gov). The Department of Energy Web site provides information on hydrogen production and uses in the United States. There are links to basic hydrogen facts; articles and fact sheets about hydrogen fuel and fuel cells; and information on hydrogen vehicle technologies (through the FreedomCAR initiative).

# Index

# Picture Credits

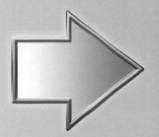

# About the Editor

David M. Haugen holds a master's degree in English from the University of Washington. He has served as the managing editor of Greenhaven Press and as a general editor for Lucent Books. He now works as a freelance writer and editor. He is the author of more than thirty young-adult, nonfiction titles.